Horace Stuart Cummings

Dartmouth College

Sketches of the Class of 1862

Horace Stuart Cummings

Dartmouth College
Sketches of the Class of 1862

ISBN/EAN: 9783337060800

Printed in Europe, USA, Canada, Australia, Japan

Cover: Foto ©ninafisch / pixelio.de

More available books at **www.hansebooks.com**

Sketches of the Class of 1862.

BY

Horace Stuart Cummings.

1 8 8 4.

WASHINGTON, D. C. :

H. I. ROTHROCK, PRINTER, 1427 F STREET, N. W.

1884.

CLASSMATES :

The class of 1862 never had any class organization while in college, and has had no meeting, organization, secretary, or records since graduation.

All we have known of each other since leaving college has been by rumor and by casual intercourse.

Believing it would be a pleasure to us who are living to know in detail the lives of our classmates, I undertook the labor of collecting the necessary information, and, as the result of much time, more patience, and nearly four hundred letters and communications, I am able to present to you this volume, which, I hope, may be pleasant reading to all.

The facts and dates are given as reported to me, and I hope they may be found correct.

I am indebted to Professor Eastman, of the Scientific class, for aid in collecting the sketches of the graduates of the Chandler School.

I especially thank those of the class who have aided me by their prompt replies, and those who have given me information concerning others.

With a sincere wish for the prosperity of "1862," I remain,

Yours truly,

HORACE STUART CUMMINGS.

Washington, D. C.,
    June 15, 1884.

FACULTY AND INSTRUCTORS

OF

DARTMOUTH COLLEGE, 1858--1862.

Rev. NATHAN LORD, D. D.,
PRESIDENT.

DIXI CROSBY, M. D.,
Professor of Surgery, Obstetrics, and Diseases of Women and Children.

Rev. ROSWELL SHURTLEFF, D. D.,
Professor Emeritus of Moral Philosophy and Political Economy.

EDWARD ELISHA PHELPS, M. D., LL. D.,
Professor of the Theory and Practice of Physic and Pathological Anatomy.

Hon. ISAAC FLETCHER REDFIELD, LL. D.,
Professor of Medical Jurisprudence.

ALBERT SMITH, M. D.,
Professor of Materia Medica and Therapeutics.

ALPHEUS CROSBY, A. M.,
Professor Emeritus of the Greek Language and Literature.

IRA YOUNG, A. M.,
Appleton Professor of Natural Philosophy and Astronomy. [Died 1858.]

OLIVER PAYSON HUBBARD, M. D.,
Hall Professor of Mineralogy and Geology, and Professor of Chemistry and Pharmacy.

Rev. CLEMENT LONG, D. D., LL. D.,
Professor of Intellectual Philosophy and Political Economy.

Rev. SAMUEL GILMAN BROWN, D. D.,
Evans Professor of Oratory and Belles Letters.

EDWIN DAVID SANBORN, A. M.,
Professor of Latin, &c. [Resigned 1859.]

Rev. DANIEL JAMES NOYES, D. D.,
Phillips Professor of Theology.

EDMUND RANDOLPH PEASLEE, M. D.,
Professor of Anatomy and Physiology.

JOHN SMITH WOODMAN, A. M.,
Professor of Civil Engineering.

Rev. JOHN NEWTON PUTNAM, A. M.,
Professor of the Greek Language and Literature.

JAMES WILLIS PATTERSON, A. M.,
Professor of Mathematics 1858-'60; Astronomy and Meteorology from 1860.

Rev. HENRY FAIRBANKS, A. M.,
Appleton Professor of Natural Philosophy from 1859.

Rev. CHARLES AUGUSTUS AIKEN, A. M.,
Professor of the Latin Language and Literature from 1859.

JOHN RILEY VARNEY, A. B.,
Professor of Mathematics from 1860.

WILLIAM ALFRED PACKARD, A. M.,
Professor of Modern Languages from 1860.

WALBRIDGE A. FIELD, A. M.,
Tutor Mathematics (1858).

CHARLES HENRY BOYD, A. B.,
Tutor Mathematics (1859–'60).

SAMUEL AUGUSTUS DUNCAN, A. B.,
Tutor of the Latin and Greek Languages from 1860.

WARREN ROBERT COCHRANE, A. B.,
Tutor of Mathematics (1861).

OLIVER PAYSON HUBBARD, A. M.,
Librarian.

DANIEL BLAISDELL, A. M.,
Treasurer.

FRESHMEN.

Name.	Residence.	Room.
Allen, Galen,	Acworth,	Mr. Watson's.
Bailey, William Frederic,	Jaffrey,	Mrs. Corey's.
Barton, Ira McLaughlin,	Newport,	Mr. J. Dudley's.
Brown, Calvin Smith,	Seabrook,	W. H., 13.
Chase, Levi Gilbert,	Loudon,	W. H., 7.
Clark, Daniel Campbell,	Orford,	Mr. Corey's.
Clark, James Adams,	Franklin,	Miss McMurphy's.
Clement, Charles Russell,	Woodstock, Vt.,	Miss Freeman's.
Collins, William Z.,	Darien, Ga.,	Mr. Richardson's.
Crane, Amos Waters,	Toledo, O.,	Mr. Pinneo's.
Cross, Oliver Lyford,	Northfield,	Miss McMurphy's.
Cummings, Horace Stuart,	Exeter,	Hanover Hotel.
Davidson, Milon,	Acworth,	Mr. Watson's.
Davis, David Franklin,	Nottingham,	Hanover Hotel, 13.
Eveleth, Frederic Wood,	Fitchburg, Ms.,	W. H., 15.
Fairbanks, William Paddock,	St. Johnsbury, Vt.,	Mr. G. W. Dewey's.
Fellows, Stark,	. East Weare,	Mr. Osgood's.
Folsom, David,	Derry,	Mr. Clifford's.
French, James,	Hartford, Vt.,	Dr. Hill's.
Gage, Nathaniel Parker,	North Hampton,	Miss Hawkins's.
Gates, Clarence Dyer,	Cambridge. Vt.,	Mr. Walker's.
Gleason, Edgar,	Thetford, Vt.,	Mr. Gove's.
Goodwin, Octavius Barrell,	Dayton, Me.,	Mr. Walker's.
Haynes, David Arthur,	Alexandria,	Mr. Osgood's.
Hubbard, Grosvenor Silliman,	Hanover,	Prof. Hubbard's.
Hunt, Simeon,	Seekonk, Ms.,	W. H., 7.
Johnson, William Edward,	Woodstock, Vt.,	Miss Freeman's.
Lake, Arthur Sewall,	London Centre,	Prof. Sanborn's.
Lamprey, Henry Phelps,	Concord,	Mr. Clement's.
Leonard, Orville Rinaldo,	Rochester, Vt.,	Miss McMurphy's.
Marden, Henry,	New Boston,	Dr. Shurtleff's.

McLeran, Benjamin,	Barnet, Vt.,	D. H., 19.
Merrill, Noah Lane,	Hopkinton,	Mr. Haskell's.
Milligan, John Wesley,	Braddock's Field, Pa.,	Mr. Walker's.
Milligan, Joseph Robert,	Braddock's Field, Pa.,	Mr. Walker's.
Morrill, George Washington,	East Weare,	Miss Freeman's.
Morris, Samuel Jones,	Rockville, Pa.,	Mr. Walker's.
Noyes, Gilman,*	Atkinson,	Miss Everett's.
Palmer, Charles Myron,	Orfordville,	Miss Freeman's.
Palmer, Edwin Franklin,	Waitsfield, Vt.,	Mrs. Douglass'.
Parker, Retire Hathorn,	Exeter,	Miss Hawkins's.
Patch, George Bela,	Hartford, Vt.,	Mr. Clement's.
Peck, William Henry,	Lyndon, Vt.,	Mr. Pinneo's.
Pember, Jay Read,	Randolph, Vt.,	Tontine.
Potter, Alvah A.,	East Concord,	Dr. Shurtleff's.
Putnam, Samuel Porter,	Pembroke,	Mr. Haskell's.
Somes, Arthur Hubbard,	Manchester,	W. H., 13.
Stevens, John Sanborn,	Hardwick, Vt.,	Miss Hawkins's.
Symmes, Algernon Sydney,	Ryegate, Vt.,	Mr. Watson's.
Town, Chauncey Warriner,	Montpelier, Vt.,	Mr. Walker's.
Walker, Augustus Chapman,	North Barnstead,	Mr. Richardson's.
Warren, John Sidney,	Wolfboro',	Mr. Pelton's.
White, Randall Hobart,	Peru, N. Y.,	T. H., 15.

FRESHMEN : 53.

* Partial course.

SOPHOMORES.

Name.	Residence.	Room.
Allen, Galen,	Acworth,	Tontine, 12.
Allen, James Franklin,	Hopkinton,	Hanover Hotei. 24.
Bailey, Frederic William,	Jaffrey,	Mrs. Powers'.
Banfield, Joshua Stuart,	Dover,	Mr. Powers'.
Bouttelle, David Emory,	Tully, N. Y.,	Mr. Osgood's.
Brown, Calvin Smith,	Seabrook,	T. H., 13.
Chase, Charles W.,	Meredith,	Mr. Osgood's.
Chase, Howard Malcolm,	Stratham,	T. H., 15.
Chase, Levi Gilbert,	Loudon,	W. H., 21.
Clark, James Adams,	Franklin,	T. H., 22.
Clement, Charles Russell,	Woodstock, Vt.,	D. H., 14.
Collins, William Z.,	Darien, Ga.,	W. H., 11.
Crane, Amos Waters,	Toledo, O.,	D. H., 20.
Cross, Oliver Lyford,	Northfield,	Mr. Carter's.
Cummings, Horace Stuart,	Exeter,	W. H., 13.
Davidson, Milon,	Acworth,	Tontine, 14.
Davis, David Franklin,	Nottingham,	Major Tenney's.
Dudley, Jason Henry,	Hauover,	Mr. Dudley's.
Emerson, Luther Wilson,	Candia,	Tontine, 10.
Eveleth, Frederic Wood,	Fitchburg, Ms.,	Mr. Powers'.
Farr, George,	Littleton,	Gates House, 3.
Fellows, George Marshall,	New Hampton,	W. H., 19.
Fellows, Stark,	East Weare,	Mr. Richardson's.
Folsom, David,	Derry,	Mr. Wainwright's.
French, James,	Hartford, Vt.,	Dr. Hill's.
Gage, Nathaniel Parker,	North Hampton,	W. H., 13.
Gates, Clarence Dyer,	Cambridge, Vt.,	Gates House, 7.
Gill, George Fuller,	Exeter,	T. H., 24.
Goodwin, Octavius Barrell,	Dayton, Me.,	Mr. Haynes'.
Haynes, David Arthur,	Alexandria,	W. H., 19.
Hobbs, George Frank,	Wakefield,	Mrs. Corey's.
Hubbard, Grosvenor Silliman,	Hanover,	Prof. Hubbard's.
Hunt, Simeon,	Seekonk, Ms.,	W. H., 21.

Ingraham, Andrew,	New Bedford, Ms.,	Mr. Dow's.
Johnson, William Edward,	Woodstock, Vt.,	D. H., 14.
Kingsbury, Josiah Weare,	Tamworth,	T. H., 15.
Lake, Arthur Sewall,	Loudon Centre,	Prof. Sanborn's.
Lamprey, Henry Phelps,	Concord,	Mr. Clement's.
Leonard, Orville Rinaldo,	Rochester, Vt.,	Mr. Dewey's.
Marden, Henry,	New Boston,	Dr. Shurtleff's.
McKowen, John,	Jackson, La.,	Mr. Watson's.
McLeran, Benjamin,	Barnet, Vt.,	D. H., 20.
Milligan, John Wesley,	Braddock's Field, Pa.,	Mr. R. Smith's.
Milligan, Joseph Robert,	Braddock's Field, Pa.,	Mr. R. Smith's.
Morrill, George Washington,	East Weare,	Mr. Richardson's.
Morris, Samuel Jones,	Rockville, Pa.,	Mr. Walker's.
Palmer, Charles Myron,	Orfordville,	Mr. Walker's.
Palmer, Edwin Franklin,	Waitsfield, Vt.,	Mr. Gilman's.
Parker, Retire Hathorn,	Exeter,	Miss Hawkins's.
Patch, George Bela,	Hartford, Vt.,	Mr. Clement's.
Peck, William Henry,	Lyndon, Vt.,	W. H., 18.
Pember, Jay Read,	Randolph, Vt.,	T. H., 24.
Potter, Alvah Kimball,	East Concord,	Mrs. Demman's.
Putnam, Samuel Porter,	Pembroke,	Mr. Haskell's.
Richardson, George Lovell,	East Medway, Ms.,	Gates House, 13.
Sanborn, John Jay,	Charlestown, Va.,	Mr. Osgood's.
Somes, Arthur Hubbard,	Manchester,	T. H., 13.
Stevens, John Sanborn,	Hardwick, Vt.,	Mr. Powers'.
Symmes, Algernon Sydney,*	Ryegate, Vt.,	Tontine.
Taylor, George Harvey,	Andover, Ms.,	Miss Freeman's.
Tebbetts, John Arthur,	Hopkinton,	Mr. Haskell's.
Tibbetts, Charles Henry,	Freyburg, Me.,	Mr. Haskell's.
Town, Chauncey Warriner,	Montpelier, Vt.,	Mr. Walker's.
Tuck, Edward,	Exeter,	Prof. Patterson's.
Walker, Augustus Chapman,	North Barnstead,	Mr. L. Dewey's.
Warren, John Sidney,	Wolfboro',	Mr. Pelton's.
White, Randall Hobart,	Peru, N. Y.,	Mr. Gilman's.
Wiggin, Augustus Wiswall,	Wakefield,	Mrs. Corey's.

SOPHOMORES : 68.

* Deceased.

JUNIOR CLASS.

Name.	Residence.	Room.
Allen, Galen,	Acworth,	Tontine.
Allen, James Franklin,	Hopkinton,	D. H.. 7.
Alvord, Augustus,	Bolton, Ct.,	T. H., 18.
Bailey, Frederic William,	Jaffrey,	Mr. Powers'.
Banfield, Joshua Stuart,	Dover,	Mr. Walker's.
Bouttelle, David Emory,	Tully, N. Y.,	Major Tenney's.
Brown, Calvin Smith,	Seabrook,	T. H., 16.
Chase, Howard Malcolm,	Stratham,	Major Tenney's.
Chase, Levi Gilbert,	Loudon,	W. H., 21.
Chase, Thomas Noyes,	West Newbury, M.,	D. H., 16.
Clark, James Adams,	Franklin,	D. H., 8.
Clarke, Stephen Wells,	Pittsfield,	Mr. Osgood's.
Clement, Charles Russell,	Woodstock, Vt.,	D. H., 14.
Crane, Amos Waters,	Toledo, O.,	D. H., 18.
Cross, Oliver Lyford,	Northfield,	Mr. Carter's.
Cummings, Horace Stuart,	Exeter,	D. H., 9.
Davidson, Milon,	Acworth,	Tontine.
Davis, David Franklin,	Nottingham,	Major Tenney's.
Dudley, Jason Henry,	Hanover,	Mr. Dudley's.
Emerson, Luther Wilson,	Candia,	D. H., 10.
Eveleth, Frederic Wood,	Fitchburg, Ms.,	T. H., 20.
Farr, George,	Littleton,	T. H., 18.
Fellows, George Marshall,	New Hampton,	W. H., 19.
Fellows, Stark,	East Weare,	Mr. Richardson's.
Follett, Harmon Dewey,	Allegan, Mich.,	Mrs. Nichols'.
Folsom, David,	Derry,	Mr. Wainwright's.
French, James,	Hartford, Vt.,	Dr. Hill's.
Gage, Nathaniel Parker,	North Hampton,	W. H., 16.
Gill, George Fuller,	Exeter,	W. H., 24.
Goodwin, Octavius Barrell,	Dayton, Me.,	Mr. Haynes'.
Hobbs, George Frank,	Wakefield,	D. H., 2.
Hubbard, Grosvenor Silliman,	Hanover,	Mrs. Chase's.
Hunt, Simeon,	Rehoboth, Ms.,	Mr. Haines'.

Ingraham, Andrew,	New Bedford, Ms.,	Mr. Dow's.
Johnson, William Edward,	Woodstock, Vt.,	D. H., 14.
Kingsbury, Josiah Weare,	Tamworth,	T. H., 12.
Lake, Arthur Sewall,	Loudon Centre,	Prof. Sanborn's.
Lamprey, Henry Phelps,	Concord,	Tontine, 9.
Leonard, Orville Rinaldo,	Rochester, Vt.,	Mr. L. Dewey's.
Marden, Henry,	New Boston,	Mr. Walker's.
McKowen, John,	Jackson, La.,	Mr. Coffee's·
McLeran, Benjamin,	Barnet, Vt.,	D. H., 18.
Milligan, John Wesley,	Braddock's Field, Pa.,	Mrs. Chase's.
Milligan, Joseph Robert,	Braddock's Field, Pa.,	Mrs. Chase's.
Morrill, George Washington,	East Weare,	Mr. Richardson's.
Morris, Samuel Jones,	Rockville, Pa.,	D. H., 11.
Palmer, Charles Myron,	Orfordville,	Mr. Walker's.
Palmer, Edwin Franklin,	Waitsfield, Vt.,	Mr. Gilman's.
Patch, George Bela,	Hartford, Vt.,	D. H., 16.
Peck, William Henry,	Lyndon, Vt.,	W. H., 24.
Pember, Jay Read,	Randolph, Vt.,	T. H., 24.
Potter, Alvah Kimball,	East Concord,	Mr. Cobb's.
Putnam, Samuel Porter,	Pembroke,	Mr. Haskell's.
Richardson, George Lovell,	East Medway, Ms.,	W H., 16.
Somes, Arthur Hubbard,	Manchester,	T. H., 16.
Stevens, John Sanborn,	Hardwick, Vt.,	Mrs. Chase's.
Taylor, George Harvey,	Andover, Ms.,	Mr. Powers'.
Tebbetts, John Arthur,	Hopkinton,	Mr. Haskell's.
Tibbetts, Charles Henry,	Freyburg, Me.,	Mr. Haskell's.
Town, Chauncey Warriner,	Montpelier, Vt.,	D. H., 11.
Tuck, Edward,	Exeter,	W. II., 17.
Walker, Augustus Chapman,	North Barnstead,	Mr. L. Dewey's.
Warren, John Sidney,	Wolfboro',	Mr. Pelton's.
White, Randall Hobart,	Peru, N. Y.,	Mr. Gilman's.
Wiggin, Augustus Wiswall,	Wakefield,	D. H., 2.

JUNIORS: 65.

Name.	Residence.	Room.
Allen, Galen,	Acworth,	Mr. Gove's.
Allen, James Franklin,	Hopkinton,	D. H.. 7.
Alvord, Augustus,	Bolton, Ct.,	T. H., 18.
Bailey, Frederic William,	Jaffrey,	Observatory.
Banfield, Joshua Stuart,	Dover,	Mr. Gilman's.
Bouttelle, David Emory,	Tully, N. Y.,	Major Tenney's.
Brown, Calvin Smith,	Seabrook,	D. H., 17.
Chase, Howard Malcolm,	Stratham,	Major Tenney's.
Chase, Levi Gilbert,	Loudon,	T. H., 19.
Chase, Thomas Noyes,	West Newbury, Ms.,	Mr. Haskell's.
Clark, James Adams,	Franklin,	D. II., 1.
Clarke, Stephen Wells,	Pittsfield,	Mr. Osgood's.
Clement, Charles Russell,	Woodstock, Vt.,	T. H., 9.
Crane, Amos Waters,	Toledo, O.,	D. H., 15.
Cross, Oliver Lyford,	Northfield,	R. H., 1.
Cummings, Horace Stuart,	Exeter,	R. H., 2.
Davidson, Milon,	Acworth,	Tontine.
Davis, David Franklin,	Nottingham,	Major Tenney's.
Dudley, Jason Henry,	Hanover,	Mr. Dudley's.
Emerson, Luther Wilson,	Candia,	R. II., 9.
Eveleth, Frederic Wood,	Fitchburg, Ms.,	R. H., 10.
Farr, George,	Littleton,	T. II., 18.
Fellows, George Marshall,	New Hampton,	R. H., 10.
Fellows, Stark,	East Weare,	Mr. Page's.
Folsom, David,	Derry,	Mr. Wainwright's.
French, James,	Hartford, Vt.,	R. H., 6.
Gage, Nathaniel Parker,	North Hampton,	R. II., 7.
Gill, George Fuller,	Exeter,	D. II., 17.
Goodwin, Octavius Barrell,	Biddeford, Me..	D. II., 6.
Hobbs, George Frank,	Wakefield,	Mr. Cobb's.
Hubbard, Grosvenor Silliman,	Hanover,	R. H., 3.
Hunt, Simeon,	Rehoboth, Ms.,	Mr. Wainwright's.
Ingraham. Andrew,	New Bedford, Ms.,	Mr. Cobb's.

Johnson, William Edward,	Woodstock, Vt.,	T. H., 9.
Kingsbury, Josiah Weare,	Tamworth,	T. H., 10.
Lake, Arthur Sewall,	Loudon Centre,	Prof. Sanborn's.
Lamprey, Henry Phelps,	Concord,	Tontine, 9.
Marden, Henry,	New Boston,	R. H., 8.
McLeran, Benjamin,	Barnet, Vt.,	D. H., 15.
Milligan, John Wesley,	Braddock's Field, Pa.,	Mrs. Chase's.
Milligan, Joseph Robert,	Braddock's Field, Pa.,	Mrs. Chase's.
Morrill, George Washington,	East Weare,	R. H., 5.
Palmer, Charles Myron,	Orfordville,	R. H., 8.
Palmer, Edwin Franklin,	Waitsfield, Vt.,	Gates House.
Patch, George Bela,	Hartford, Vt.,	Mr. Haskell's.
Peck, William Henry,	Lyndon, Vt.,	W. H., 24.
Pember, Jay Read,	Randolph, Vt.,	T. H., 24.
Potter, Alvah Kimball,	East Concord,	Mrs. Brown's.
Richardson, George Lovell,	East Medway, Ms.,	R. H., 7.
Somes, Arthur Hubbard,	Manchester,	Mr. Currier's.
Stevens, John Sanborn,	Hardwick, Vt.,	Observatory.
Taylor, George Harvey,	Andover, Ms.,	Mrs. Chase's.
Town, Chauncey Warriner,	Montpelier, Vt.,	D. H., 11.
Tuck, Edward,	Exeter,	W. H., 17.
Warren, John Sidney,	Rochester,	R. H., 1.
White, Randall Hobart,	Peru, N. Y.,	Gates House.
Wiggin, Augustus Wiswall,	Wakefield,	D. H., 12.

SENIORS : 57.

CHANDLER

SCIENTIFIC DEPARTMENT.

FOURTH CLASS.

Name.	Residence.	Room.
Bartholomew, Henry Luzerne,	Fowler, Ill.,	Mr. Cobb's, 1.
Douglass, Charles Lee,	Hanover,	Mrs. Douglass'.
Ferguson, Alfred Harrison,	South Berwick, Me.,	Gates House, 13.
Fessenden, William Henry,	Boston, Ms.,	Mr. Haynes'.
Heilge, Charles Curtis,	Boston, Ms.,	Mr. Haynes'.
Livingston, Augustus,	Lowell. Ms.,	Mrs. Shattuck's.
Morse, James Wellman,	New York City.	Mrs. Morse's.
Potter, Wilkins Updike,	Coventry, R. I.,	Mrs. Douglass'.
Sanborn, Josiah Bean,	Tamworth,	Mr. Carpenter's.
Staples, John A.,	Biddeford. Me.,	Mrs. Douglass'.
Thompson, Charles William,	Barnstead,	Mr. Wainwright's.
Wadsworth, Alden Bradford,	Hiram, Me.,	Mr. Corey's.

FOURTH CLASS: 12.

THIRD CLASS

Name.	Residence.	Room.
Aldrich, Wm. H. Harrison,	North Scituate, R. I.,	Mr. Cobb's.
Baldwin, William Henry,	Nashua,	Gates House, 15.
Bartholomew, Henry Luzerne,	Fowler, Ill.,	Mrs. Douglass'.
Bingham, Charles Edward,	Claremont,	Mr. Pinneo's.
Church, William B.,	Frankfort, Ky.,	Mr. Walker's.
Darling. George Edward,	St. Stephen, N. B.,	Miss Freeman's.
Douglass, Charles Lee,	Hanover,	Mrs. Douglass'.
Fellows, Charles Melroy,	Northumberland,	Mrs. Corey's.
Ferguson, Alfred Harrison,	South Berwick,	Mrs. Corey's.
Ferris, Valentine Penniman,	Swanton, Vt.,	Gates House, 6.
Fessenden, William Henry,	Boston, Ms.,	Mr. Gove's.
Furniss, William Henry,	Williamsburg, N. Y.,	Mrs. Douglass'.
Gould, James Payson,	Phillipston, Ms.,	Mr. Walker's.
Heilge, Charles Curtis,	Boston, Ms.,	Mr. Rand's.
Hopkins, John,	Gloucester, Eng.,	Elm Cottage.
Livingston, Augustus,	Lowell, Ms.,	L. H., 5
Potter, Wilkins Updike,	Coventry, R. I.,	Mrs. Douglass'.
Staples, John A.,	Biddeford, Me.,	Mr. Pinneo's.
Thompson, Charles William,	Barnstead,	Mr. Wainwright's.
Wadsworth, Allen Bradford,	Hiram, Me ,	Mrs. Corey's.
Welles, Samuel,	Glastenbury, Ct.,	Miss Freeman's.
Young, Edward Bentley,	Reading, Ms.,	Mr. L. Dewey's.

THIRD CLASS : 22.

SECOND CLASS.

Name.	Residence.	Room.
Baldwin, Wm. H. Harrison,	Nashua,	T. H., 2.
Bartholomew, Henry Luzerne,	Fowler, Ill.,	Mrs. Douglass'.
Darling, George Edward,	St. Stephen, N. B.,	L. H., 5.
Douglass, Charles Lee,	Hanover,	Mrs. Douglass'.
Eastman, John Robie,	Andover,	Gates House, 12.
Fellows, Charles Melroy,	Northumberland,	Mrs. Corey's.
Ferris, Valentine Penniman,	Swanton, Vt.,	Gates House.
Gould, James Payson,	Phillipston, Ms.,	Mr. Powers'.
Haskins, Leander Miller,	Rockport, Ms.,	Mrs. Corey's.
Heilge, Charles Curtis,	Boston, Ms.,	Mr. Rand's.
Hopkins, John,	Gloucester, Eng.,	L. H., 5.
Potter, Wilkins Updike,	Coventry, R. I.,	Mr. Wainwright's.
Staples, John A.,	Biddeford, Me.,	Mr. Haynes'.
Welles, Samuel,	Glastenbury, Ct.,	Mrs. Corey's.
Young, Edward Bentley,	Reading, Ms.,	Mr. Haskell's.

SECOND CLASS: 15.

FIRST CLASS.

Name.	Residence.	Room.
Baldwin, William Henry,	Nashua,	T. H., 1.
Darling, George Edward,	St. Stephen, N. B.,	L. H., 5.
Eastman, John Robie,	Andover,	Gates House.
Fellows, Charles Melroy,	Northumberland,	Mrs. Corey's.
Ferris, Valentine Penni-		
man,	Swanton, Vt.,	Gates House.
Gould, James Payson,	Phillipston, Ms.,	Mr. Powers'.
Haskins, Leander Miller,	Rockport, Ms.,	Gates House.
Heilge, Charles Curtis,	Boston, Ms.,	Mr. Richardson's.
Hopkins, John,	Gloucester, Eng.,	Mr. G. W. Dewey's.
Staples, John A.,	Biddeford, Me.,	Mr. Haynes'.
Welles, Samuel,	Glastenbury, Ct.,	Mr. Haynes'.
Young, Edward Bentley,	Reading, Ms.,	Academy, 8.

FIRST CLASS : 12.

PUBLIC SOCIETIES.

CLASS OF 1862.

THEOLOGICAL SOCIETY.

G. Allen,	J. W. Kingsbury,
J. F. Allen,	A. S. Lake.
A. Alvord,	H. P. Lamprey.
J. S. Banfield,	H. Marden,
H. M. Chase,	B. McLeran,
T. N. Chase,	C. M. Palmer,
W. Z. Collins,	E. F. Palmer,
A. W. Crane,	G. B. Patch,
M. Davidson,	A. K. Potter,
L. W. Emerson,	G. L. Richardson.
D. Folsom.	A. H. Somes.
J. French,	J. S. Stevens,
N. P. Gage,	A. C. Walker.

HANDEL SOCIETY.

[1862.]

D. Folsom,	N. P. Gage,
W. H. Fessenden,	O. R. Leonard,

A. C. Walker.

SCYLLA BOAT CLUB

[1862.]

Boat pulls six oars ; Built by Reed, of Charlestown.

C. W. Town, *1st Coxswain.*   C. R. Clement, *2d Coxswain.*

G. W. Morrill, *Purser.*

C. S. Brown,	O. B. Goodwin,
J. A. Clark,	W. E. Johnson,
O. L. Cross,	J. W. Milligan,
S. Fellows,	S. J. Morris,
C. D. Gates,	S. P. Putnam,

G. H. Taylor.

SCIENTIFIC DEPARTMENT.

PHILOTECHNIC SOCIETY.

[1862.]

W. H. Baldwin,	J. P. Gould,
G. E. Darling,	L, M. Haskins,
J. R. Eastman,	J. Hopkins,
C. M. Fellows,	J. A. Staples,
V. P. Ferris,	S. Welles,

E. B. Young.

SECRET SOCIETIES

OF

DARTMOUTH COLLEGE.

CLASS OF 1862.

PSI UPSILON.

Charles W. Chase,
Stephen W. Clarke,
Oliver L. Cross,
Luther W. Emerson,
Arthur D. Haynes,

George F. Hobbs,
Henry P. Lamprey,
Henry Marden,
Edwin F. Palmer,
Retire H. Parker,

Samuel P. Putnam,
Edward Tuck,
John S. Warren,
Augustus W. Wiggin.

KAPPA KAPPA KAPPA.

Levi G. Chase,
Thomas N. Chase,
George Farr,
Stark Fellows,
Simeon Hunt,

Orville R. Leonard,
John C. McKowen,
John W. Milligan,
Joseph R. Milligan,
George W. Morrill,

Samuel J. Morris,
George B. Patch,
Chauncey W. Town,
Augustus C. Walker.

ALPHA DELTA PHI.

James F. Allen,   G. S. Hubbard,   Alvah K. Potter,
Frederick W. Bailey, Arthur S. Lake,   John J. Sanborn,
David E. Bouttelle, Benjamin McLeran,   John S. Stevens,
Amos W. Crane,   Charles M. Palmer,   George H. Taylor.

DELTA KAPPA EPSILON.

Augustus Alvord,   Horace S. Cummings, William E. Johnson,
Calvin S Brown,   David F. Davis,   William H. Peck,
Howard M. Chase,   Fred. W. Eveleth,   George L. Richardson,
James A. Clark,   David Folsom,   Arthur H. Somes.
Charles R. Clement, Nathaniel P. Gage,

ZETA PSI.

Galen Allen,   James French,   Josiah W. Kingsbury,
Joshua S. Banfield, John A. Tebbetts,   J. Read Pember,
Milon Davidson,   Charles H. Tebbetts, Randall H. White.
Harmon D. Follett,

CHANDLER DEPARTMENT.

PHI ZETA MU.

William H. Aldrich,   Charles M. Fellows,   Edward B. Young.

SIGMA DELTA PI.

William H. Baldwin,
H. L. Bartholomew,
Charles E. Bingham,
William B. Church,
George E. Darling,
Charles L. Douglass,
John R. Eastman,

Alfred H. Ferguson,
Valentine P. Ferris,
Wm. H. Fessenden,
James P. Gould,
Leander M. Haskins,
Charles C. Heilge,
Samuel Welles,

John Hopkins.
Augustus Livingston,
Wilkins U. Potter,
John A. Staples,
Charles W. Thompson,
Alden B. Wadsworth.

PHI BETA KAPPA.

S. W. Clarke,
H. S. Cummings,
M. Davidson,
S. Fellows,

D. Folsom,
G. S. Hubbard,
S. Hunt,
A. S. Lake,

C. M. Palmer,
J. S. Stevens,
E. Tuck.

SOPHOMORE SUPPER.

CLASS OF '62,

HANOVER HOTEL, JULY 20, 1860.

MUSIC: MANCHESTER CORNET BAND.

PRESIDENT..........JOHN S. STEVENS.	VICE PRESIDENT..OCTAVIUS B. GOODWIN.
ORATOR·...........CALVIN S. BROWN.	MARSHAL...........JOHN J. SANBORN.
POET ....GEORGE B. PATCH.	TOAST MASTER....GEO. L. RICHARDSON.

Committee of Arrangements,

SAM. J. MORRIS,   JOHN W. MILLIGAN,   EDWARD TUCK,

GEORGE H. TAYLOR,   GROSVENOR S. HUBBARD.

CLASS DAY.

DARTMOUTH COLLEGE,

July 29, 1862.

EXERCISES.

THE CLASS WILL ENTER THE

COLLEGE CHURCH

AT 3 O'CLOCK, P. M.,

DAVID FOLSOM, Marshal,

Derry, N. H.

PRAYER BY PROF. J. W. PATTERSON.

MUSIC.

ORATION.. EDWARD TUCK,

Exeter, N. H.

MUSIC.

POEM...RANDALL H. WHITE,
Peru, N. Y.

MUSIC.

CHRONICLES.....................................JAMES A. CLARK,
Franklin, N. H.

MUSIC.

PROPHECIES...............................AUGUSTUS W. WIGGIN,
Wakefield, N. H.

ODE...JASON H. DUDLEY,
Hanover, N. H.

The Class will then move in procession to the President's house.

ADDRESS......................................OLIVER L. CROSS,
Northfield, N. H.

Thence proceeding to the

"OLD PINE"

an address will be delivered by

BENJAMIN MCLERAN, Barnet, Vt.

MUSIC BY THE GERMANIA BAND.

ORDER OF EXERCISES

AT

COM·MENCEMENT,

DARTMOUTH COLLEGE,

July 31, 1862.

ORDER OF EXERCISES.

PRAYER.

MUSIC.

The following Speakers were Selected from the Class by Lot.

---

1. The Modern Tendency to Equality.
   AMOS WATERS CRANE, Toledo, Ohio.

2. The best Historians not mere Students.

CHARLES MYRON PALMER, Orfordville.

3. The Advantages and Temptations of Self-taught Men.

CHARLES RUSSELL CLEMENT, Woodstock, Vt.

4. Sensibility to Public Opinion.

WILLIAM HENRY PECK, Lyndon, Vt.

5. The Moral and Practical Bearings of Direct Taxation.

HORACE STUART CUMMINGS, Exeter.

MUSIC.

6. Distinguished Talent Developed by Great Crises.

GEORGE LOVELL RICHARDSON, East Medway, Ms.

7. Scottish Character.

GEORGE HARVEY TAYLOR, Andover, Ms.

8. The Rights of Uncivilized Nations.

JOHN SIDNEY WARREN, Rochester.

9. Popular Inconsiderateness the Great Danger of States.

JAMES FRENCH, Hartford, Vt.

10. Count Cavour.

GEORGE MARSHALL FELLOWS, New Hampton.

MUSIC.

11. Heroism.

MILON DAVIDSON, Acworth.

12. American Nationality as Affected by the Civil War.
GEORGE FARR, Littleton.

13. The Present Fields of Geographical Discovery.
FREDERICK WOOD EVELETH, Fitchburg, Mass.

14. The American Navy.
OCTAVIUS BARRELL GOODWIN, Biddeford, Me.

15. The Personal Discipline of the Orator.
JAY READ PEMBER, Randolph, Vt.

MUSIC.

16. Do States Inevitably Tend to Decay?
JOSHUA STUART BANFIELD, Dover.

17. The Effects of Commerce on Civil Liberty.
JAMES FRANKLIN ALLEN, Hopkinton.

18. The Liberalizing Influence of College Studies.
JOSEPH ROBERT MILLIGAN, Braddock's Field, Pa.

19. The Scholar-Statesmen of England.
JOHN SANBORN STEVENS, Hardwick, Vt.

20. The Dicipline of Nations.
FREDERICK WILLIAM BAILEY, Jaffrey.

MUSIC.

AN ORATION IN ENGLISH.

21. Scholars in Revolutions.
Mr. ALBERT CORNELIUS PERKINS, Topsfield, Ms.

A Candidate for the Degree of Master of Arts.

MUSIC.

———

DEGREES CONFERRED.

———

MUSIC.

———

PRAYER.

GRADUATES.

DR. GALEN ALLEN, RED WING, MINN.

Galen Allen, son of Winslow and Nancy (Grout) Allen, was born at Chelsea, Vt., August 2, 1833. His father was a farmer. He fitted at New London, N. H., and entered college in the fall of 1858 and continued through the course.

At graduation he was a Democrat; a Congregationalist; paid his own college expenses, and intended to follow teaching as a profession.

After graduation he was principal of Chelsea (Vt.) Academy to Spring of 1863; principal of Grammar School at Milford, Mass., to Fall of 1865; same of High School at Nantucket, for two years, to Fall of 1867; principal of High School at Bath, Me., to 1874; studied medicine in mean time with Dr. Wm. E. Payne; attended medical lectures at Hanover in 1874, and at the Boston University in 1875, where he graduated the same year. Commenced practice at Boston, but soon removed to Red Wing, Minn., where he has since resided; has a good practice, and has been successful.

He is Independent in politics and "Apostolic" in creed.

Married Miss Lucy A. Gage, at East Washington, N. H., April 20, 1867.

Children: Annie G. Allen, nat., February 3, 1868.
Harry W., nat., July 10, 1872.
Mary G., nat., January 9., 1879.

JAMES FRANKLIN ALLEN, Esq., Washington, D. C.

James Franklin Allen, son of Jonathan Leach and Caroline Brown (Allison) Allen, was born at Hopkinton, N. H., August 13, 1841. His father was a farmer. He fitted at Hopkinton and Pembroke (N. H.) Academies, and entered college in the Fall of 1859 and continued through the course.

At graduation he was 6-feet ½-inch in height; 175 pounds in weight; brown hair; light complexion; a Congregationalist; a Republican; paid his own college expenses; intended to become a lawyer.

After graduation he taught the High School at Bradford, N. H., from 1862 to December, 1863, reading law the while with Hon. Mason W. Tappan. December 23, 1863, he was appointed to a clerkship in the Third Auditor's office, U. S. Treasury, Washington; he attended the Columbian Law School, graduating LL. B., June 11, 1866, and admitted to the bar the same month; resigned his position under Government January 1, 1876, and engaged in the practice of law until March, 1881, when he was appointed to a position in the Adjutant General's office, which he resigned February 14, 1882, and was appointed the same day to a position in the Indian office, where he now remains. He retained his legal residence at Bradford, N. H., until January 1, 1876; he now has his legal residence at Rockville, Md. He is prominent in Masonic circles and has taken many of the higher degrees. He made the trip across the Continent in the Summer of 1883. Is a Republican, but would like to see another party of the old "Know Nothing Party" principles; is a member of the Lutheran church.

Married Miss Julia A. Dow, at Washington, D. C., October 25, 1866.

No children.

Rev. AUGUSTUS ALVORD, Prescott, Mass.

Augustus Alvord, son of Martin and Martha B. (Clark) Alvord, was born at Bolton, Conn., August 31, 1834. His father was a farmer. He fitted at Monson, Mass., and entered Amherst College in the class of '62, and entered the class of '62, Dartmouth, in the Spring of 1860, and continued through the course.

At graduation he was 5-feet 11-inches in height; 170 pounds in weight; had light brown hair; full beard; paid his own college expenses; a Congregationalist; a Republican, and intended to become a minister.

After graduation he taught the High school at Lisbon, N. H., to the Spring of 1863; entered the Theological Seminary at Hartford, Conn. in the Spring of 1863, and continued to the Autumn of the same year, when he, November, 1863, enlisted in the 1st Connecticut Heavy Artillery, and served to January, 1865, when he was appointed and commissioned Chaplain in the 31st U. S. Colored Troops; he was present at Appomattox at the surrender of Lee : then the regiment was ordered on duty in Texas, where he was mustered out November, 1865; he preached in Texas the following six months, and then returned North, and supplied the church at Marlboro', Vt., in 1866-7; preached at Ridgebury, Conn., 1867-71; West Suffield, Conn., and Cummington, Mass., 1871-74; West Granville, Mass., 1874-79; Braintree, Vt., 1879-80; Hillsboro', N. H., 1880-81; and installed at Prescott, Mass., as pastor of the Congregationalist church, in May, 1881, and so continues. He is a Republican.

Married to Miss Laurestine A. Hartwell, of Lisbon, N. H., September 6, 1866. Second: Miss Emily A. Parsons, at West Granville, Mass., January, 1876.

Children : Mable A., nat., July, 1872.

Frederick P., nat., June, 1878.

FREDERICK WILLIAM BAILEY.

Frederick William Bailey, son of Captain Edward and
Sarah (Hayden) Bailey, was born at Jaffrey, N. H.,
August 15, 1838. His father was a manufacturer. He
fitted at Appleton Academy, New Ipswich, N. H., and
entered college in the Fall of 1858, and continued
through the course.

At graduation he was 5-feet 10½-inches in height; 160
pounds in weight; had light brown hair; chin whiskers;
light complexion; paid his own college expenses; Congregationalist; Republican, and intended to become a
lawyer.

After graduation he taught the Richmond (Me.) Academy in 1862–3; read law in the office of Wheeler ¸&
Faulkner, at Keene, N. H., from October, 1863, to November, 1864, when he entered the Albany (N. Y.) Law
School, and was admitted to the New York bar May 4,
1865, and to that of New Hampshire in October, 1865;
he represented the town of Jaffrey in the N. H. Legislature in 1864–5; began practice at East Jaffrey in March
1866, and continued until January 1, 1870, when he removed to Keene, N. H. He again represented Jaffrey in
the State Legislature in 1868–9. He lived but a short
time after removing to Keene, as he was taken with a
fatal attack of diptheria, and died April 27, 1870, at
Keene, N. H.

Bailey was one of the most promising men of the class
while in college, and he gave evidences in his subse-
quent life of future success, which was only prevented
by his early death.

He married Miss Mary Perkins, of Jaffrey, at Hinsdale,
N. H., September 2, 1866, who died December 8, 1867.

Children: Mary Fredericka, nat., December 6, 1867,
who is living at East Jaffrey with relatives.

JOSHUA STUART BANFIELD, Esq., Boston, Mass.

Joshua Stuart Banfield, son of Joshua and Esther Parkman (Hart) Banfield, was born at Dover, N. H., September 16, 1840. His father was a merchant. He fitted at the Franklin Academy, Dover, and entered college in the Spring of 1859, and continued through the course.

At graduation he was 5-feet 4-inches in height; 125 pounds in weight; black hair; side whiskers; light complexion; Congregationalist; a Republican, and intended to become a minister.

After graduation he taught the Rochester (N. H.) Academy, 1862-3; the High School at Scituate, Mass., 1863-4; then became a teacher and Superintendent under the auspices of the New England Freeman's Aid Society at Petersburg, Va., March, 1864, to September, 1864; at Alexandria, Va., to July, 1865; at Norfolk, Va., and Columbus, Ga., to February, 1867; then returned to Boston and engaged in business as real estate and commercial broker until 1868. From 1868 to 1875, he was employed continuously on the staff of the " *Boston Evening Traveler* "; from 1875 to date, he has been one of the editorial and business staff of the " *Boston Journal of Commerce,*" and so continues. He is a Republican and Congregationalist.

Married Miss Harriette Rosevelt Smith, at Brooklyn, N. Y., October 1, 1867.

Children: Henry Stuart, nat., May 20, 1875. Florence Harriette, nat., November, 23, 1878.

DAVID EMERY BOUTTELLE.

David Emery Bouttelle, son of David Bartlett and Anna (Hobart) Boutelle, was born at Tully, N. Y., October 27, 1837. He entered college in 1859, and continued through the course.

At graduation he was 5-feet 6-inches in height; 138 pounds in weight; had dark brown hair; light complexion; side whiskers; paid his own college expenses; a Congregationalist; Republican; intended to become a lawyer.

After graduation he taught at Marcellus, N. Y., from Fall of 1862, to the Spring of 1863; he remained at home for one year, being much impaired in health, going to the sea shore in the Summer of 1864, where he derived some benefit. He taught at Liverpool, N. Y., from the Fall of 1864 to the Fall of 1865; principal of the Cortland Academy, at Homer, N. Y., from Fall of 1865 to Fall of 1866; principal of Grammar School at Unionville, Conn., from Fall of 1866 to Spring of 1869, when his health again failed him, and he returned to his home at Tully.

During the Summer of 1870, he visited his friends in Connecticut, and took a trip up the New England coast, when he returned home and remained there until the time of his death, which occurred July 5, 1871.

He was a successful teacher, and made many warm friends; he was an honest, true man, and a faithful friend.

He never married.

COL. CALVIN SMITH BROWN, WASHINGTON, D. C.

Calvin Smith Brown, son of Newell and Abigail P. (Leavitt) Brown, was born at Seabrook, N. H., January 4, 1837. His father was a farmer and stock raiser. He fitted at New London, N. H., and entered college in the Fall of 1858, and continued through the course.

At graduation he was 6-feet in height; 170 pounds in weight; had black hair; side whiskers and mustache;

dark complexion; smoked; a Congregationalist; Republican, and intended to become a lawyer. While in the Junior year, he enlisted in the Seventh Squadron of Rhode Island Cavalry for three months' service.

After graduation he was Captain in the 17th Regiment New Hampshire Volunteers from December, 1862, to April, 1863; read law with Hon. Aaron Hayden, of Eastport, Me., to March, 1865, when he was appointed Captain in the Maine Volunteers; promoted to be Lieutenant-Colonel of the 1st Battalion of Maine Infantry in May, 1865; was in command of five districts of South Carolina in latter part of same year; mustered out of service in April, 1866.

He then returned to his law studies at Eastport, Me., and was admitted to the bar in October, 1866; removed to St. Louis, Mo., in the December following, and practiced law to the Spring of 1870; removed to Montgomery County, Kansas, and engaged in law; member of the Kansas Legislature in 1873; Mayor of Parker, Kansas, in 1874-5-6; removed to city of Coffeyville, Kansas, in 1877; was Mayor in 1878; removed to the East in 1879, and was appointed to a position in the General Land Office at Washington, D. C., which he still holds.

He claims to be an anti-monopoly Republican, and approximating Universalism in creed.

Married Miss Carrie Noyes Witherell, at Eastport, Me., November 15, 1871.

Children: Annie W., nat., July, 1874; ob. August, 1874.
Sarah W., nat., September 2, 1877.
Edith L., nat., March 29, 1881.

HOWARD MALCOLM CHASE.

Howard Malcolm Chase, son of Elisha and Sarah

(Jewell) Chase, was born at Stratham, N. H., October 17, 1839. His father was a farmer. He fitted at Phillips Exeter Academy, and entered college in the Fall of 1859, and continued through the course.

At graduation he was 6-feet 2-inches in height, 155 pounds in weight; had brown hair, light complexion, paid his own college expenses; a Baptist, Republican, and intended to become a lawyer.

After graduation he felt it to be his duty to aid his Country, and at once enlisted in the 15th Regiment New Hampshire Volunteers, and went with the regiment to Louisiana and engaged in the campaign against Port Hudson, he was taken down with disease and ordered to his home, but died on the way, at Memphis, Tenn., August 16, 1863.

Chase entered the service out of the purest patriotism, was a good soldier, and died a martyr for his country.

He was a man of unexceptionable character in all things.

Rev. LEVI GILBERT CHASE, CONCORD, N. H.

Levi Gilbert Chase, son of Jonathan and Phebe (Page) Chase, was born at Loudon, N. H., April 30, 1840. His father was a farmer. He fitted at the Friend's School at Providence, R. I., and at Thetford, Vt., and entered college in 1858, and continued through the course.

At graduation he was 5-feet 8-inches in height, 137 pounds in weight; had brown hair, light complexion; was a Republican, a Congregationalist; undecided as to future vocation.

After graduation he taught at Wentworth, N. H., in 1862, and then traveled in the West; entered Andover Theological Seminary in September, 1863, and remained to December, 1864; was in the service of the Christian Commission in Virginia and West Virginia, from January, 1865, to the close of the war; taught in Hermann, Gasconade County, Mo., in winter of 1865-6; was licensed to preach in June, 1867, and preached at Jamaica, Fayetteville, and Dummerstown, Vt., from August, 1867, to January, 1870.

Attended lectures at Andover Seminary in 1870, and was ordained pastor at Dummerstown, August 24, 1870, where he remained to December, 1878; preached at Guildhall, Vt., until December, 1879; then removed to his former home in Loudon, his health being impaired, and supplies churches there and in the neighboring towns, as his health permits. He is a Congregationalist and a Republican.

He never married.

PROFESSOR THOMAS NOYES CHASE, ATLANTA, GA.

Thomas Noyes Chase, son of Samuel Sewall and Eunice Noyes (Colby) Chase, was born at West Newbury, Mass., July 18, 1838. His father was a farmer and lumber dealer. He fitted at Thetford (Vt.) Academy, and entered Amherst College in 1859, and entered the class of '62, Dartmouth, in 1860, and continued through the course.

At graduation he was 5-feet 8-inches in height, 150 pounds in weight; had auburn hair, chin whiskers, sandy complexion; smoked; was a Congregationalist, a Democrat, and intended to become a minister.

After graduation he was principal of Royalton (Vt.) Academy, from 1862 to 1864. From 1864 to 1869, he resided in Washington, D. C., first as City Missionary for a few months, then was appointed a Corresponding Clerk in the U. S. Post-Office Department, teaching private pupils in Greek and Latin in the mean time, and studying theology with Dr. Samson, President of Columbian College. From 1869 to date he has been professor of Greek in Atlanta (Ga.) University, but has been absent from active duty at various times on account of impaired health and for other reasons. For fifteen months he was the Government Agent for the Indians of the Green Bay Agency, Wisconsin. Engaged one year in general work for the American Missionary Association, in the South. Was absent six months in inspecting the Mendi Mission on the West Coast of Africa, between Sierra Leone and Liberia, visiting, on the way, Liverpool, London, Paris and Funchal. Spent about two years in planning and superintending the construction of school buildings at Atlanta and Macon, Ga., and Mobile and Talladega, Ala., New Orleans, La., Austin, Texas, Tougaloo, Miss., and Nashville, Tenn., erected from the fund of $150,000, given by the late Mrs. Valeria G. Stone, of Malden, Massachusetts, to the Am. Missionary Association, and from other funds. He is a Republican and Congregationalist. He is one of the most important officers in the Atlanta University.

He married Miss Mary Maria Tuttle, of Acton, Mass., at Thetford, Vt., August 1, 1862.

Children : Mary, nat., August 12, 1863, (now in the senior year Wellesley College.
John Hildreth, nat., October 25, 1874.
Frank Paul, nat., October 18, 1875, ob. July 9, 1876.

JAMES ADAMS CLARKE, Esq., WATERLOO, WIS.

James Adams Clarke, son of Joseph and Lucy Jane (White) Clarke, was born at Randolph, Vt., July 23,

1842. His father was a merchant and manufacturer. He fitted at Franklin, N. H., and entered college in the Fall of 1858, and continued through the course.

At graduation he was 5-feet 8½-inches in height, 150 pounds in weight; had black hair, light complexion, smoked; was a Republican, a Roman Catholic, and intended to become a lawyer.

After graduation he immediately commenced the study of law with his uncle, Hon. Austin F. Pike, at Franklin, N. H., and was admitted to the bar at Concord in 1865, and practiced law with Mr. Pike for two years. His hearing became seriously impaired in 1864, so much so that he was obliged to give up the practice of law—doing so in 1867, and removed to Waterloo, Wis., and engaged in farming, in which he has been eminently successful. To speak for himself, he says: "am pleasantly situated, have a very good farm, plenty of leisure, go off fishing every year, am quite comfortable generally, and always delighted to see a Dartmouth man."

He is "ouden" in politics, and Roman Catholic in creed.

(I must say that I am under many obligations to him for his great interest in this compilation of the Class History, and for much valuable information that he has given me; in fact he has shown more interest in the matter than any other member of the class.—H. S. C.)

Married to Miss Mary J. Hughes, at Ashland, N. H., July 31, 1865.

Children : Mary Lucy, nat., December 5, 1868.

Charles Joseph,
Martha Charlotte, } twins, nat., August 7, 1870.

Martha Charlotte ob. September 10, 1877.

STEPHEN WELLS CLARKE, MANCHESTER, N. H.

Stephen Wells Clarke, the son of John and Asenath (Wells) Clarke, was born at Pittsfield, N. H., June 30, 1837. His father was a merchant and farmer. He fitted at Phillips Exeter Academy, and entered College in 1858 (in the class of 1861), and afterwards entered the class of '62 in 1859, and continued through the course.

At graduation he was 5-feet 8½-inches in height; weighed 135 pounds; had black hair, chin whiskers and dark complexion, smoked, paid his own college expenses ; was a Congregationalist, Republican in politics, and intended to become a teacher.

After graduation he was teacher of Greek and Mathematics at Nichols Academy, Dudley, Mass., from 1862 to 1865. He then removed to Portsmouth, N. H., and was teacher in the Boy's High School at that place from 1865 to 1874; principal of the United High School of Portsmouth from 1874 to 1881, when he was compelled to give up teaching on account of impaired health. In 1881 he removed to Manchester, N. H., where he is engaged in the jewelry business--the firm being " Clarke & Dixon," 877 Elm street. Clarke reports himself as in improved health, and prosperous in business. He is a Mason and Knight Templar, and also an Odd Fellow ; a Republican, and of the Methodist Episcopal creed.

He married Miss Jane Annie Hill, at Portsmouth, May 5, 1868.

Children : Marion Hill, nat., February 25, 1869.

Gertrude Wells, nat., January 26, 1875.

CHARLES RUSSELL CLEMENT, Esq.

Charles Russell Clement, son of Rev. Jonathan and Phebe Foxcraft (Phillips) Clement, was born at Chester,

N. H., November 8, 1840. He fitted at Kimball Union (Meriden) Academy, and entered college in the Fall of 1858, and continued through the full course.

At graduation he was 5-feet 7-inches in height, 135 pounds in weight; had dark brown hair, chin whiskers, light complexion, smoked; was a Congregationalist, a Republican, and intended to become a lawyer.

After graduation he was appointed to a clerkship in the Treasury at Washington, which he retained until 1865, when he returned to his home at Woodstock, Vt., and commenced the study of law in the office of French & Johnson; he was soon appointed assistant clerk of the County Court, and was the acting clerk till July, 1867; in July, 1867, he was appointed to a responsible clerical position in the Superintendent's office of the Pennsylvania Railroad at Altoona, Pa., which he held a few weeks only, when he was appointed chief clerk of the office of Superintendent of Transportation ; in 1870 he was appointed the Division Superintendent of the Pullman Palace Car Company, at Jersey City; in November, 1871, he was made the advertising agent of the Pennsylvania Railroad Company; from this position he was promoted to the responsible place of General Baggage Agent, having charge of all matters connected with the transportation of baggage on all the lines of the Pennsylvania Railroad Company east of Pittsburg and Erie.

Under his skillful management the loss and damage to baggage was reduced to the minimum, and his success in settling claims and tracing lost articles, was notable in railroad circles. As an example, during the Centennial Exhibition, in 1876, although the Pennsylvania Railroad moved 1,384,966 pieces of baggage that year, they had to pay only $167.69 on account of baggage destroyed or damaged, and only $1,739.30 for baggage lost or stolen, and the management of the company highly complimented Mr. Clement for the great ability displayed by him in his official duties.

He was very popular and a general favorite in all circles, and a successful future was predicted for him.

He was taken with a severe, and, as it proved, a fatal illness of but a few weeks duration, and died at Philadelphia, January 8, 1881.

He was buried in West Laurel Hill Cemetery, on the banks of the Schuylkill.

He was never married.

The *Railway Journal*, at the close of a long notice of his life and death, says : " The memory of ' Charley Clement ' will be tenderly cherished in the New England home of his earlier years, as well as in the State of his adoption, where the prime of his life was passed."

AMOS WATERS CRANE, Esq., East Toledo, Ohio.

Amos Waters Crane, son of Gabriel and Mary Ann (Whitmore) Crane, was born at Toledo, Ohio, November 7, 1837. His father was a farmer. He fitted at Toledo, and entered college in the Fall of 1858, and continued through the full course.

At graduation he was 5-feet 3-inches in height, 129 pounds in weight; had dark complexion, black hair; was a Republican, a Baptist, and intended to become a teacher.

After graduation he returned to his home at Toledo, and engaged in farming which he has since followed, leading a quiet and useful life. He is still a Baptist and a Republican.

He married Miss Emma Cook, at Toledo, March 22, 1865.

Children : Alice, aged 17 ; Fidelia, aged 15 ; Edward, aged 13 ; Fanny C., aged 6. Two have deceased.

OLIVER LYFORD CROSS, Esq., NORTHFIELD DEPOT, N. H.

Oliver Lyford. Cross, son of Jeremiah and Sarah (Lyford) Cross, was born at Northfield, N. H., June 11, 1836. He fitted at Sanbornton Bridge, N. H., and entered college in the Fall of 1858, and continued through the course. His father was a farmer.

At graduation he was 5-feet 10-inches in height, 140 pounds in weight ; had dark brown hair, full beard, dark complexion, smoked ; was a Congregationalist, Democrat, and intended to become a lawyer.

After graduation he taught in Hanover, N. H., in the Winter of 1862–3 ; studied law with Pike & Barnard, at Franklin, N. H., and was admitted to practice at Concord, in 1865, and began practice in Franklin ; spent much of the year 1866, in traveling in the West, and located at Montgomery City, Mo., where he engaged in the practice of law January 1, 1867 ; was City Attorney, and Mayor of Montgomery. On the death of his father he returned to his old home, at Northfield, in 1873, where he has since resided, engaged in law business and also in farming. He still adheres to his former political and religious creeds. Is a Mason and Knight Templar.

He married Miss Lucy R. Hill, of Northfield, at Tilton, N. H., November 14, 1866. Mrs. Cross is a brilliant scholar, and delivered a poem at the Centennial of Northfield, in 1880, which has since been published.

Children : Arthur Benson, nat., May 29, 1868.

Robert Lee, nat., January 26, 1872.

Evelyn Montgomery, nat., January 6, 1875.

HORACE STUART CUMMINGS, Esq., WASHINGTON, D. C.

Horace Stuart Cummings, son of Rev. Jacob (Dart.
1819) and Harriot (Tewksbury) Cummings, was born at
Southborough, Mass., July 1, 1840. His father was a
Congregational minister. He fitted at Phillips Exeter
Academy, and entered college at the Fall term of 1858,
and continued through the full course.

At graduation he was 5-feet 9-inches in height, 175
pounds in weight, had dark brown hair, light complexion, smoked ; was a Republican, a Congregationalist, and
intended to become a lawyer.

After graduation he at once began the study of law
with Hon. Charles H. Bell (Dart. 1844), at Exeter, with
whom he had previously studied law during two Winter
vacations.

He entered the Albany, N. Y., Law School in August,
1863, and was admitted to the New York bar by examination in December, 1863 ; continued the study of law
in New York City until May, 1864, when he returned to
his home in Exeter and began practice.

He was appointed to a position in the Treasury Department, at Washington, D. C., in February, 1865,
which he retained until the Summer of 1873, when he
resigned and entered upon the practice of the law at 1411
F Street, and so continues.

He retains his legal residence in New Hampshire, and
was the Assistant Secretary of the New Hampshire Sen-
ate in 1863 and 1864, and Secretary of the same 1865 and
1866 ; represented the town of Exeter in the New Hampshire Legislature in 1876 and 1877, and was Chairman of
the Committee on Elections, and was permanent Chairman of the Republican Legislative Caucus ; was Aide on
the Staff of the Governor in 1877, with the rank of
Colonel.

He spent most of the years 1870 and 1871, in traveling for pleasure in Europe, visiting most of the important points.

He is connected with quite a number of incorporations as president, treasurer, counsel, &c. He is a member of the New Hampshire Historical Society, and of the New England Historic-Genealogical Society.

He has no reason to complain, and thinks that the world has treated him as well as the average—and, perhaps, better than he has deserved.

He still adheres to his former religious and political belief.

He married Miss Jeannette E. Irvin, at Pittsburg, Pa., October 15, 1874.

No children.

MILON DAVIDSON, ESQ., NEWFANE, VT.

Milon Davidson, son of Alvan and Ann (Howe) Davidson, was born at Unity, N. H., November 28, 1834. His father was a farmer. He entered college in the Fall of 1858, and continued through the course.

At graduation he was 5-feet 6½-inches in height, 148 pounds in weight, had dark brown hair, dark complexion; paid his own college expenses, was a Democrat, a Congregationalist, and intended to become a minister.

After graduation he was the principal of the Bath (N. H.) Academy, to Summer of 1863; taught Select School at Worcester, Vt., to Summer of 1864; principal of the Northfield (Vt.) Academy, to Summer of 1865; principal of the Franklin (Vt.) Academy, to Summer of 1866; same at Henniker, N. H., in the Fall of 1866; at the Wilson (N. Y.) Academy, 1866-7; then associate principal of the New Hampton Literary Institution, Fairfax,

Vt., for one year, and principal of the same for one and
one-half years, when he resigned and began the study of
law in Fairfax; in 1870, removed to Townsend, Vt., and
was principal of the Leland & Gray Seminary for four
years; during this last period he continued the study of
the law, and was admitted to practice in the Fall of 1872;
that same year he was made Treasurer of the Windham
County Savings Bank, and still continues, which office
and his law business occupy his entire time.

He is a Democrat, a Baptist, and prominent in tem-
perance organizations.

Married Miss Gratia E. Andrews, at Richmond, Vt.,
November 28, 1864.

Children : Lula E., nat., May 29, 1866.

DAVID FRANKLIN DAVIS, Esq., Waco, Texas.

David Franklin Davis, son of Jacob and Anna (Davis)
Davis, was born at Nottingham, N. H., November 25,
1832. His father was a farmer. He fitted at Phillips
Exeter Academy, and entered college in the Fall of 1858,
and continued through the course.

At graduation he was 5-feet 7½-inches in height, 150
pounds in weight, had black hair, full beard, dark complexion, smoked ; liberal in creed, a Democrat, and intended to become a lawyer.

After graduation he taught a school near Cincinnati,
Ohio, for one year with good success ; from 1863 to 1865,
he was connected with the Quartermaster's Department,
U. S. Army, principally at Washington.

In 1865, he went to Texas as an assistant to collect the
United States direct tax, and has resided in Waco, that
State, ever since. He became actively engaged in the
politics of the State, and became Justice of the Peace

for McLennan County, Clerk of the District Court, and
Probate Judge of the same county from 1870 to 1874;
presided over the State Republican Convention in 1869,
when Gov. E. J. Davis was nominated and elected, the
last victory for the Republican party of Texas.

He is now engaged in the United States Postal Service.
He owns a large hotel in Waco, which he leases, and has
been snccessful in a financial way. He is an out and out
Republican, and thinks that all the Democrats of the
North would become Republicans if they could be transferred to Texas for one or two years. He is liberal in
creed, with a leaning towards Spiritualism.

He has kept alive the poetic fire that he evinced at college in the shape of many poetical effusions, one of
which is before me, named the "East Line Zephyrs,"
descriptive of the progress and enterprise of his adopted
State, and in speaking of himself, says:

"In the classic halls of Dartmouth,
This Davis once hath trod,
Back to historic England,
He traces up his blood."

He married Miss Sophie F. L. Wiebusch, at Waco, February 4, 1873.

Children : Franklin H. J., nat., December 16, 1873;
ob. February 14, 1874.
Olive J. L., nat., August 14, 1874.
Jennie Lee, nat., May 7, 1879.
Walter Lamar, nat., February 23, 1881.

JASON HENRY DUDLEY, COLEBROOK, N. H.

Jason Henry Dudley, son of Jonathan and Minerva
(Armstrong) Dudley, was born at Hanover, N. H., No-

vember 24, 1842. His father was a farmer. He fitted
for college at Hanover, and entered the Spring term of
1859, and continued through the course.

At graduation he was 5-feet in height, 110 pounds in
weight; had light hair and complexion, smoked, Episcopalian in creed and Democratic in politics, and intended
to become a teacher.

After graduation he was principal of Colebrook (N.
H.) Academy, from 1862 to 1865, reading law at the same
time with Hon. W. S. Ladd; principal of Danville (Vt.)
Academy, 1865 and 1866, and studied law with Hon.
Bliss N. Davis; principal of the West Randolph (Vt.)
Academy, 1866 and 1867, and reading law with Hon.
Edmund Weston, and was admitted to the Supreme
Court of Vermont, at Chelsea, December, 1867.

He then went to Colebrook and entered into the practice of his profession, and has so continued, having won
a good reputation as a lawyer and gained a profitable
practice.

He has held many town offices, and has held the position of State Attorney for Coos County for three terms,
and still holds it. He still remains a Democrat, and of
the Episcopalian creed.

He married Miss Lucy A. Bradford, of Vergennes, Vt.,
September 22, 1869.

Children : Allen B. Dudley, nat., June 18, 1870.
William H. Dudley, nat., April 13, 1871 ;
ob. July 2, 1874.

LUTHER WILSON EMERSON, Esq., NEW YORK CITY.

Luther Wilson Emerson, son of Hon. Abraham and
Abigail (Dolbear) Emerson, was born at Candia, N. H.,
October 14, 1838. His father was a farmer. He fitted

at Phillips (Andover) Academy, and entered college in
the Spring of 1859, and continued through the course.
At graduation he was 5-feet 5-inches in height, 130
pounds in weight, had black hair, dark complexion, full
beard; paid his own college expenses, was a Congregationalist, a Republican, and intended to become a lawyer.
After graduation he was the principal of the Muncie
(Ind.) Academy, from September, 1862, to the Fall of
1863; principal of the State Street Grammar School, at
Columbus, Ohio, from Fall of 1863 to April 1865; then
went to New York City and taught, and in the year 1866,
began the study of law in the office of Lewis & Cox,
(Hon. S. S. Cox,) and was admitted to the Supreme
Court bar in April, 1867, and entered upon practice.
In March, 1868, he was appointed Assistant U. S. Attorney in the office of the United States District Attorney
for the Southern District of New York, and held the position until January 1, 1873; since that time he has been
in active practice, with good success, at 149 Broadway;
he resides at 125 Gates Avenue, Brooklyn.
He is generally Republican, with a tendency to Electi-
cism, and a firm believer in New England Orthodoxy.
Says: "that his experience in New York confirms his
predilections in favor of Hell—and a good deal of it—
for those who seemingly escape all punishment in this
life, and that there must be a balancing of accounts some-
where to complete my sense of exact and equal justice."
Married Miss Anna Melvina Sharpe, at Columbus,
Ohio, December 29, 1870.
Children : Harold S., nat., November 9, 1871.
        Luther L., nat., Aug. 3, 1874.
        Nannie M., nat., September 4, 1877.
        Marian D., nat., August 9, 1881.

FREDERICK WOOD EVELETH, Esq., Montgomery, Ala.

Frederick Wood Eveleth, son of John Henry and
Martha (Holman) Eveleth, was born at Farmington, Me.,
December 16, 1840. His father was a merchant. He
fitted at the High School at Fitchburg, Mass., and entered college in 1858, and continued through the course.
At graduation he was 5-feet 7½-inches in height, 146
pounds in weight, had dark brown hair, light complexion, side whiskers; was a Congregationalist, a Republican, and undecided as to future vocation.

After graduation he remained for some time at his
home at Fitchburg, and in 1865 he went to Idaho in the
employ of the "Northern Mining Company," of which
company he was a member.

In 1867 he returned to the East by way of Oregon,
California, and Panama, and opened a private school at
Havre de Grace, Maryland, in which he was quite successful. In 1870 he returned to Fitchburg, where he was
principal of the Day Street Grammar School to 1875 ;
was principal of the High School at Saugus, Mass., to
1879, when he went to Colorado, and engaged in hotel-
keeping at Monument, and was also interested in mining.
He made an extended tour in Europe, in 1878; in 1881
he removed to West Virginia and engaged in teaching
at Raleigh Court House; in 1882 he was appointed principal of the "Swayne School," at Montgomery, Ala.,
where he still remains. He is of his former political
and religious creeds.

He married Miss Mary L. Hanscom, of Auburn, Me.,
at that place, July 10, 1874.

No children.

CAPTAIN GEORGE FARR, LITTLETON, N. H.

George Farr, son of John and Tryphena (Morse) Farr, was born at Littleton, N. H., February 12, 1836. His father was a lawyer. He fitted at Thetford (Vt.) Academy, and entered Amherst College, and remained one year, when he entered Dartmouth at the beginning of Sophomore year, and continued through the course.

At graduation he was 5-feet 9½-inches in height, 154 pounds in weight, had black hair, dark complexion, full beard; a Congregationalist, Republican, and intended to become a lawyer.

After graduation he enlisted in the 18th Regiment New Hampshire Volunteers, and was commissioned Captain and served with his company until June 1, 1864, when he was wounded in the charge at the battle of Coal Harbor; remained in hospital until February, 1865, when he was put on Court-martial duty at Norfolk, Va., until the close of the war. His wounds did not heal until the Winter of 1867. After his return home he engaged in the manufacture of starch until 1867; then went into trade until 1873, when he sold out; in 1870 he was appointed Deputy Sheriff, and in 1873-4, he devoted himself entirely to his official duties; in October, 1874, he bought the Oak Hill House, a Summer hotel at Littleton, which he has conducted ever since, having greatly enlarged and beautified the same; has been Justice of the Littleton Police Court; and Collector of Taxes, and member of the Board of Education for nine years.

He intended becoming a lawyer, but his severe wound, together with sunstroke, so injured his health, that he had to give it up. He is of the same political faith, and his creed is the "Golden Rule"; is a Mason.

Married Miss Eliza C. Boynton, at Springfield, Mass., January, 1871.

Children : Grace Emma, nat., December 3, 1871.
    Gertrude T., nat., October 15, 1873.
    Leslie B., nat., December 1, 1878.

GEORGE MARSHALL FELLOWS, Esq., Boston, Mass.

George Marshall Fellows, son of Calvin Peterson and
Mary Jane (Worthen) Fellows, was born at Bristol, N.
H., May 8, 1837. His father was a farmer. He fitted at
New Hampton, N. H., and entered college in the Fall of
1859, and continued through the course.

At graduation he was 5-feet 8-inches in height, 150
pounds in weight; had dark brown hair, side whiskers,
sandy complexion, smoked; a Methodist, Republican,
and undecided as to future vocation.

After graduation he was principal of the High School
at Contoocookville, N. H., to November, 1862; then
principal of the High School at Franklin, N. H., to May,
1865; taught at the Academy, at Corinth, Vt., and at
the Falley Seminary, N. Y., each for a short time; then
was in business at Lawrence, Mass., until June, 1868;
then principal of the Avery School, at Dedham, Mass.,
until August, 1871; principal of the Blake School, at
Hyde Park, and afterward principal of the " Grew "
School, from which position he was made Sub-master of
the Dorchester Everett School, in Boston, which position
he still occupies. His residence is in Hyde Park.

He says that he has prospered in his profession, and
feels that he is doing some good. He is a Mason, a Republican, and a Methodist.

Married Miss Ellen Maria Emmons, at Bristol, N. II.,
August 12, 1862.

Children: Calvin Peterson, nat., September 17, 1863.
    Horace Emmons, nat., January 5, 1865.

Edward St. Clair, nat., December 29, 1866.

Frank Marshall, } twins, nat., July 24,
George Frederick, }   1874.

COL. STARK FELLOWS.

Stark Fellows, son of Rufus and Sarah Ann (Silver) Fellows, was born at Sandown, N. H., April 15, 1840. His father was a merchant. He entered college in the Fall of 1858, and continued through the course.

At graduation he was 5-feet 7-inches in height, 165 pounds in weight; had black hair, side whiskers and mustache, light complexion, smoked; no religious preferences, Democrat, and intended to become a lawyer.

After graduation he enlisted in the 14th Regiment New Hampshire Volunteers, and was made 2d Lieutenant October 9, 1862; resigned September 4, 1863; went before United States Military Board, and passed a competitive examination for a field officer's position—he received the highest marking, and was appointed Lieutenant-Colonel of the 2d United States Colored Troops. He was in command of Fort Taylor, Key West, Florida, when he was taken down with the yellow fever; he became convalescent, but a relapse coming on he died May 23, 1864.

Stark Fellows had a quick and brilliant mind, and had he lived, would have become a man of note and influence.

He never married.

DAVID FOLSOM, Esq., NEW YORK CITY.

David Folsom, son of Hon. John and Dorothy (Underhill) Folsom, was born at Chester, N. H., January 4, 1839. His father was a farmer, and also Judge of the

Probate Court. He fitted at Williston Seminary, East-
hampton, Mass., entered college in the Fall of 1858, and
continued through the course.

At graduation he was 5-feet 9-inches in height, 150
pounds in weight; had brown hair, light complexion,
chin whiskers; paid his own college expenses; Congregationalist, Republican, and undecided as to future vocation.

After graduation he at once entered commercial pursuits in connection with his brothers, who were prominent merchants. He was in business in Memphis, Tenn.,
from 1862 to 1863; at New Orleans, from 1863 to 1864;
at St. Louis, from 1864 to 1866; at New York City, from
1866 to the present time—the firm being that of H. & D.
Folsom, 15 Murray Street.

Since being in business in New York he has resided at
Dobbs Ferry, on the Hudson, in 1866-7; at Orange, N.
J., in 1867-77; and since that date in New York City.

He is a Republican, and a Protestant Episcopalian.

He has traveled much in Europe, having crossed the
Atlantic twelve times.

He married Miss Eleanor Titus, at Providence, R. I.,
December 21, 1865. She died at New York City, October 7, 1883. A great loss to her husband and son.

Children : David Folsom, nat., October 25, 1868.

JAMES FRENCH, Esq., BOSTON, MASS.

James French, son of Moses and Almira (Herrick)
French, was born at Meadville, Pa., October 21, 1839.
His father was a merchant. He fitted at Kimball Union
Academy, Meriden, N. H., and entered college in the
Fall of 1858, and continued through the course.

At graduation he was 6-feet in height, 165 pounds in

weight; had brown hair, light complexion, chin whiskers; a Congregationalist, Republican, and undecided as
to future vocation.

Since graduation he has been engaged in commercial
business entirely, having been in business in Boston, from
1863 to 1867; Burlington, Iowa, from 1867 to 1871; Louisville, Ky., from 1871 to 1879; St. Louis, from 1879 to
1881; Chicago, Ill., from 1881 to 1883; Boston, from
1883 to date.

He says: " have been seeking my fortune since leaving college, in mercantile pursuits, and am still flirting
with the fickle dame with final results doubtful."

He is Independent in politics, and attends the Episcopal
church.

He married Miss Emma J. Day, at Portland, Me., January, 1869.

Children: Margaret Clare, nat., November, 1870; died
        January, 1876.
        James McDonald, nat., September, 1877.
        Roberta S., nat., February, 1880; ob. June,
        1880.

NATHANIEL PARKER GAGE, Esq., WASHINGTON, D. C.

Nathaniel Parker Gage, son of Samuel Kimball and
Myra (Parker) Gage, was born at Pelham, N. H., April
26, 1838. His father was a shoe manufacturer. He fitted
at Phillips Andover Academy, entered college in the Fall
of 1858, and continued through the course.

At graduation he was 5-feet 10-inches in height, 155
pounds in weight; had black hair, full beard, dark complexion, paid his own college expenses; a Congregationalist, Republican, and undecided as to future occupation.

After graduation he became a teacher, and has followed
that profession ever since.

He taught at North Hampton, N. H., to March, 1864;
Ripon, Wis., to August, 1866; Fort Atkinson, Wis., to
August, 1867; Prescott, Wis., to July, 1868; Lake For-
est, Ill., to July, 1869; Mystic River, Conn., to July,
1870, when he removed to Washington, D. C., where he
has since resided.

He was principal of the Seaton School to 1874, and
since that date, has been, and is, Supervising Principal of
Schools, having ninety-two schools under his charge.

He has the reputation of being an able and valuable
instructor.

He says that his sympathies are with the Republicans,
but is disfranchised by reason of his residence in the District of Columbia. Is a Congregationalist.

He made the tour of Europe in 1878. Is still a bache-
lor, and there are symptoms of its becoming chronic.

DR. GEORGE FULLER GILL, ST. LOUIS, MO.

George Fuller Gill, son of Charles and Deborah Ann
(Belcher) Gill, was born at Farmington, Me., February
5, 1843. His father was a sea captain and merchant. He
fitted at Phillips Exeter Academy, entered college in the
Fall of 1859, and continued through the course.

At graduation he was 5-feet 10-inches in height, 145
pounds in weight; had black hair, dark complexion,
smoked; a Congregationalist, a Democrat, and intended
to become a lawyer.

After graduation he at once entered the military service as hospital steward in a regiment of Rhode Island
cavalry; attended Harvard Medical School in 1862-3;
was appointed a United States Medical Cadet in March,

1863, and was on duty at St. Louis, and pursued his
medical studies at the Medical College of the University
of St. Louis, graduating M. D., in March, 1864; at that
date he was made Acting Assistant Surgeon of the Army
at Madison General (Army) Hospital in Indiana, and so
continued to the close of the war in July, 1865, when he
left the service and settled in the practice of medicine at
St. Louis, where he has since resided.

He was in the frontier service in the Indian campaign
of the Winter of 1869-70, as Surgeon to the 5th and 10th
regiments United States Cavalry. He is now one of the
medical staff of St. Luke's hospital at St. Louis. His address is 610, N. 4th street.

Traveled extensively in Europe in 1873-4, and in 1882.

He is not married. In politics he is rather indefinite,
but styles himself as " American "; and in religion an
Episcopalian.

OCTAVIUS BARRELL GOODWIN, ESQ., OIL CITY, PA.

Octavius Barrell Goodwin, son of John Marston and
Mehitabel Walker (Day) Goodwin, was born at Hollis,
Me., July 22, 1840. He fitted at Phillips Andover Academy, entered college in the Fall of 1858, and continued through the course.

At graduation he was 5-feet 11-inches in height, 150
pounds in weight; had dark brown hair, light complexion, side whiskers; Unitarian in creed, Democrat, undecided as to future vocation.

After graduation he engaged in mercantile business in
North Carolina; returned to Maine in 1864; went to Oil
City, Pa., in 1865, and has lived there ever since. He is
engaged in real estate and machinery business—such as

engines, boilers, and steam pumps. Has been a member
of the city council, and president of the water and gas
commission of the city.

He writes that he thinks of leaving Oil City in the
present year, and, probably, going farther West. He is
still a Democrat, and attends the Episcopal church.

He married Miss Gertrude Murdoch, of Philadelphia,
Pa., May 2, 1871.

Children : Frederick D., nat., September 18, 1873.
George K., nat., September 9, 1881.

GEORGE FRANK HOBBS, Esq., Dover, N. H.

George Frank Hobbs, son of Josiah Hilton and Rhoda
Davis (Chapman) Hobbs, was born at Wakefield, N. H.,
May 6, 1841. His father was a lawyer. He fitted at
Phillips Exeter Academy, entered college in the Fall of
1859, and continued through the course.

At graduation he was 6-feet in height, 170 pounds in
weight; had dark brown hair, chin whiskers, smoked,
paid his own college expenses ; Liberal in creed, Republican, and intended to become a lawyer.

After graduation he read law with Hon. Charles Ches-
ley, at Wakefield, and with Jordan & Rollins, at Great
Falls, until September, 1864, when he enlisted in the 1st
New Hampshire Heavy Artillery ; was discharged by
special order, and was made 1st Lieutenant and Adjutant of the 18th New Hampshire Regiment (Infantry) in
October, 1864 ; served until the Spring of 1865, when he
was obliged to resign on account of ill health ; he then
returned to Wakefield and resumed his legal studies—as
far as his impaired health would permit ; after remaining
a few years at that place, he removed to Dover, and was
connected with the Hon. S. M. Wheeler, in the practice

of law for about one year, when he engaged in the practice alone, and gained a very high position at the New
Hampshire Bar, and gathered a large and profitable practice. His success was remarkable, and his labor unceas-
ing—so much so, that his health became most seriously
impaired in 1879 by overwork, and since then he has
been obliged to give up all business.

He was director in the Strafford National Bank, and
trustee of the Strafford County Savings Bank.

Married Miss Emma J. Christie, daughter of Hon.
Daniel M. Christie (Dart. 1815), at Dover, November, 18,
1873.

No children.

GROVESNOR SILLIMAN HUBBARD, Esq., NEW YORK.

Grovesnor Silliman Hubbard, son of Professor Oliver
Payson and Faith Wadsworth (Silliman) Hubbard, was
born at Hanover, N. H., October 10, 1840. His father
was Professor in Dartmouth College. He fitted at Phillips Andover Academy, entered college in the Fall of
1858, and continued through the course.

At graduation he was 5-feet 10½-inches in height, 155
pounds in weight; had brown hair, light complexion;
Congregationalist in creed, a Republican, and undecided
as to future vocation.

After graduation he taught at Grand Ligne, Canada,
from October, 1862, to March, 1863; May, 1863, to July,
1865, he held an appointment in the Register's Office,
Treasury Department, Washington; September, 1865, to
September, 1866, was in the Yale Law School; studied
law with Man & Parsons, New York City, until October,
1869; also attended Columbia Law School, and was admitted to practice in May, 1867. Practiced law by him-

self from October, 1869, to May, 1873 ; then formed
the partnership of Chittenden & Hubbard ; dissolved this
partnership in May, 1881, and since that time has been
alone in business at 35 Wall Street. He has a fine business.

Still retains the same religious and political belief ; is a
member of the University Club.

Has traveled quite extensively in Europe, having spent
the Summers of 1877 and 1878, and the Winter of 1879
traveling there.

Never married.

Dr. SIMEON HUNT, East Providence, R. I.

Dr. Simeon Hunt, son of William D. and Lydia (Chase)
Hunt, was born at Seekonk, Mass., April 27, 1837. His
father was a farmer. He fitted at the Friends' School,
Providence, R. I., and entered college in 1858, and continued through the course.

At graduation he was 5-feet 7½-inches in height, 138
pounds in weight; had dark brown hair, chin whiskers,
light complexion ; a Congregationalist, Republican, and
intended to become a doctor of medicine.

After graduation he studied medicine with Drs. Dixi
and A. B. Crosby, at Hanover, and Dr. Buck, at Manchester; attended lectures at Hanover, and took degree
of M. D. there in the Fall of 1864 ; was appointed Assistant Surgeon U. S. A. (colored troops), at graduation,
but was taken down with inflammatory rheumatism, and
was not mustered into service on that account.

Commenced practice at Corry, Pa., in February, 1865,
and after remaining there three months, removed to
Springfield, Pa., and entered into a large country practice, but was obliged to return East in the Spring of 1868,

on account of the ill health of his wife. He then settled at East Providence, and still resides there. He has a large practice and is doing well; is a member of various medical societies, and is an F. & A. M.; has traveled extensively in the Northern States and the British Possessions; made the trip of Europe in the Summer of 1877. He had invested largely in the drug business in 1874, and was burned out in 1877, losing some $10,000 besides his library. Is a Republican, and his religion the " Golden Rule."

Married Miss Anna M. Balch, of Lyme, N. H., October 25, 1865.

Children : Charles Balch, nat., September 2, 1866 ; ob. October 27, 1866.

William W., nat., April 22, 1868.

Charles Balch, nat., July 24, 1869 ; ob. August 21, 1869.

Fred. Balch, nat., January 8, 1872; drowned August 10, 1882.

Archie J., nat., November 3, 1878.

ANDREW INGRAHAM, Esq., NEW BEDFORD, MASS.

Andrew Ingraham, son of Robert and Phebe (Coffin) Ingraham, was born at New Bedford, Mass., December 19, 1841. He fitted at New Bedford, and entered college in 1859, and continued through the course.

At graduation he was 5-feet 10-inches in height, 135 pounds in weight; had dark brown hair, dark complexion, smoked ; was Liberal in creed, a Republican, and intended to become a teacher.

After graduation he soon enlisted in Company I 3d Regiment Massachusetts Volunteers; was on detached service in the Signal Corps most of the time while in service; discharged in 1863. Was principal of Plymouth, Mass., Academy in 1865–6, and is now teacher and principal in the Friends' Academy, at New Bedford, Mass. Married Miss Mary Eva Hunt, of Providence, R. I.

[Ingraham is the only graduate of '62, who has not given a sketch of himself, saying that he did not feel disposed to furnish any information.—H. S. C.

WILLIAM EDWARD JOHNSON, Esq., WOODSTOCK, VT.

William Edward Johnson, son of Eliakin and Harriet Augusta (Collamer) Johnson, was born at Woodstock, Vt., June 26, 1841. His father was a banker. He fitted at Kimball Union Academy, Meriden, N. H., and entered college in 1858, and continued through the course.

At graduation he was 6-feet, 1½-inches in height, 165 lbs. in weight; had light brown hair; light complexion; smoked; a Congregationalist, Republican, and intended to become a lawyer.

After graduation he at once began the study of law at Woodstock, with Washburn & Marsh, and was admitted to the bar at the May term, 1865; commenced the practice of law at Woodstock, July 1, 1865, with Hon. Warren C. French, under firm name of French & Johnson; this continued till December 1, 1867, when they dissolved, and Johnson has since been in practice alone at Woodstock.

He was State Attorney from 1872 to 1874, and a director in the Woodstock National Bank since 1875. He is of the same politics and creed as formerly.

Married Miss Elizabeth M. Hatch, of Woodstock, August 20, 1866.

Children : Margaret Louise, nat., October 17, 1869.

REV. JOSIAH WEARE KINGSBURY, DEERFIELD, N. H.

Josiah Weare Kingsbury, son of Rev. Samuel and Mary (Badcock) Kingsbury, was born at Underhill, Vt., October 2, 1838. He fitted at Phillips Exeter Academy, and entered college in 1859, and continued through the course.

At graduation he was 5-feet 10-inches in height, 155 pounds in weight; brown hair, chin whiskers; paid his own college expenses; Congregationalist, a Republican, and intended to become a minister.

After graduation he was the principal of the classical department of the City school at Schenectady, N. Y.; entered Princeton Theological Seminary in the fall of 1863, and continued there nearly two years, leaving on account of trouble with his eyes; preached at Eden, Vt. some four months in the summer of 1864; installed pastor of the Congregational Church at Quechee, Vt., June 28, 1866, where he had already preached one year, and so continued till September 28, 1869, when he was dismissed at his own request, in order to accept a call to North Woodstock, Conn., where he remained till April 1, 1871; he supplied the First Church at Biddeford, Me., from October, 1871 to October, 1872; installed at North Reading, Mass., October 16, 1872, and remained till April, 1877; acting pastor of the Congregational Church at Montague, Mass., from August, 1877 to April, 1879; acting pastor of the Congregational Church at Rye, N. H. from November 1, 1879 to May, 1882; in September, 1882, removed to Exeter, N. H., and has since supplied the churches in Derby and Charleston, Vt., returning to Exeter in October, 1883.

He has published some very pleasant sketches.

He accepted a call to Deerfield, N. H., in February, 1884. · He is still a Republican.

Married Miss Mary H. Jackson, at Tamworth, N. H.,
October 2, 1865.

Children : William Josiah, nat., November· 10, 1866.
        Joseph Jackson, nat., August 5, 1868.
        Samuel, nat., September 14, 1870.
        George Dean, nat., July 26, 1872.
        Mabel Hope, nat., July 19, 1874.
        Mary Lizzie, nat., Feb. 9, 1876.
        Noah, nat., January 10, 1878.
        Grace Ethel, nat., July 30, 1881.

ARTHUR SEWELL LAKE, Esq. SHENANDOAH, Iowa.

Arthur Sewell Lake, son of David and Julia B. (Sanborn) Lake, was born at Chichester, N. H., November
11, 1837. His father was a farmer. He fitted at Pittsfield, N. H., and entered college in the fall of 1858, and
continued through the full course.

At graduation he was 6-feet in height, 150 pounds in
weight; black hair, light complexion; paid his own college expenses; a Republican, a Congregationalist, and
undecided as to future vocation.

After graduation he was principal of the Conway,
(Mass.) Academy in 1862; taught at Bradford, Mass., in
1863; Higham, Mass., in 1864; Hanover, Mass., 1865;
Thomaston, Conn., 1865-1870; Winsted, Conn., 1871;
Walcottville, Conn., 1872; in 1873 he removed to Shenandoah, Iowa, where he has since resided; engaged in
the hardware business for two years, and since in the
real estate and loan business.

He was Mayor of Shenandoah in 1874, and has been a
member of the School Board. He is a Congregationalist
and a Republican.

Married to Miss Jennie H. Fox, at Thomaston, Conn.,
November 18, 1869.
Children : Carrie H. nat., September 16, 1870.
John F., nat., November 16, 1873.
Arthur, nat., January 31, 1879, ob. Feb-
ruary 5, 1879.
George F., nat., May 8, 1881, ob. January
31, 1882.

REV. HENRY PHELPS LAMPREY, CONCORD, N. H.

Henry Phelps Lamprey, son of Ephraim and Bridget
(Phelps) Lamprey, was born at Groton, N. H., November 3, 1832. His father was a farmer. He fitted at New
Hampton, N. H., and entered college in 1858, and continued through the course.

At graduation he was 5-feet 8-inches in height, 155
pounds in weight; auburn hair, full beard, dark complexion ; paid his own college expenses ; was a Free-will
Baptist in creed, Republican, and intended to become a
minister.

After graduation he was employed by the American
Tract Society, from 1862 to 1864 ; then studied divinity
at the Free Baptist Theological School at New Hampton, from 1864 to 1866; then pastor of the Free Baptist
Church at Phillips, Me., from 1866 to 1868; pastor at
Wilmot, N. H., from 1868 to 1871 ; at Brunswick, Me.,
1871-'72; East Corinth, Me., 1872-'73; South Parsons-
field, Me., 1873 to 1876 ; Northwood, N. H., 1876 to
1878. In 1878 he transferred his ecclesiastical standing
to the Congregational Church, and was pastor of the
church at West Stewartstown, N. H. in 1878-'79 ; at
Danbury, N. H., 1879 to 1881, when, on account of the
failing health of a brother, he returned to his old home

at Concord, and took charge of his business, and is at
present carrying on an extensive market garden at that
place.

He is a Republican and of the Congregationalist creed.
He married Miss Nellie S. Hardy, at New Hampton,
July 11, 1867.

Children : Lunette Emeline, born April 17, 1869.
Elmira Adrienne, born October 21, 1873.

BENJAMIN McLERAN, Esq., NEW ORLEANS, LA.

Benjamin McLeran, son of William and Eliza (Gleason) McLeran, was born at Barnet, Vt., February 5, 1840.
His father was a farmer. He fitted at Peacham, Vt., and
entered college in the fall of 1858, and continued through
the course, and was the recorder of the sins and transgressions of the class of '62 for four years, known as
class monitor.

At graduation he was 5-feet 7-inches in height, 150
pounds in weight ; had black hair, mustache, dark complexion ; paid his own college expenses ; a Republican, a
Presbyterian, and intended to become a minister.

After graduation he entered the U. S. Navy, in the
war of the rebellion, and served faithfully for two years ;
then entered the service of the Engineer Corps of the
Army of the Gulf, and was topographical engineer on
the staff of Gen. Canby at the close of the war ; he was
a teacher at Shreveport, La., under the auspices of the
Freedmen's Bureau, in 1866-'67 ; in latter year he was
elected member of the State Constitutional Convention,
representing the parish of Caddo, then resumed his profession of civil engineering and has pursued the same
ever since, having been engaged on many important surveys, and on nearly every projected railroad in the State ;

surveyor of Ouachita parish two years, division engineer
of the N. O. Mobile and Texas R. R. in 1869-'70; State
engineer of levees in 1871-'72; land surveyor in 1873-'76;
chief draughtsman of Board of State Engineers in 1876;
draughtsman to Surveyor General's office, 1877-'80 ; civil
engineer in New Orleans since that date.

He resides 107 Thalia street. He is a member of
the N. O. Academy of Sciences, of the Society of Civil
Engineers of the Gulf States, and of the N. O. Sanitary
Association ; is a Republican, and an Unitarian in creed.

Married Miss Martha M. Fitts, of Saratoga, N. Y., at
New Orleans, in 1870.

Children : Rhoda, nat., 1871

Rev. HENRY MARDEN, MARASH, CENTRAL TURKEY.

Henry Marden, son of Samuel and Phebe (Noyes)
Marden, was born at New Boston, N. H., December 9,
1837. His father was a farmer. He fitted at Francestown and Mont Vernon, (N. H.) academies, and entered
college in the fall of 1858, and continued the full course.

At graduation he was 5-feet 7½-inches in height, 135
pounds in weight; sandy hair and complexion ; paid his
own college expenses; was a Republican, a Presbyterian,
and intended to become a minister.

After graduation he taught at Bradford, Mass., 1862-'4;
at the Hitchcock Academy, Brimfield, Mass., 1864-'6 ;
studied divinity at Andover Theo. Seminary till 1869;
ordained a Congregational minister at Francestown, September 2, 1869; at once went as missionary to Aintab,
Central Turkey, under the auspices of the American
Board, having general oversight of the Central Turkey
Missions; returned to this country in July, 1875, and
remained until October, 1878, engaged in ministerial

work; then he returned to Turkey and was stationed at Marash, where he has since resided. He has the supervision of some twenty-five Protestant congregations, besides being a teacher and trustee in the Theological Seminary at Marash. He was of important service to the cause of humanity and Christianity during the terrible scenes that occurred in Central Turkey in the years of 1878-9, when the city of Zeitoon, which has a population of 10,000 christians, was in open rebellion against the Turkish Government, being driven to beggary and desperation by the merciless exactions and extortions of the Turkish rulers, who make it a point to rob the Christian population. A large force of troops was on its way to destroy Zeitoon and its inhabitants, being impelled by love of plunder and hatred of Christianity, when Mr. Marden was asked by the English Consul and the Turkish Governor at Aleppo to go to Zeitoon and seek to adjust the difficulties without bloodshed. He at once started with two native guides, on his hazardous mission for Zeitoon, which is situated among the wild peaks of the upper Taurus; the way was infested by Moslem robbers, brigands and outlaws, but he passed them all and entered Zeitoon in safety, and after holding a conference with the outlaws and rebels for one week he succeeded in adjusting their wrongs to such a degree that they capitulated and signed pledges of loyalty. When he started on his return, the soldiers, impatient to attack the Christians at Zeitoon, were making demonstrations to that end. The lives of the 10,000 Christians being imperiled, he sent a messenger on a hazardous ride of 130 miles on horseback, through a wild country and amidst bitter foes, to Aleppo, in order to report his successful mission before the army could make any attack, and thus prevent any movement. The messenger reached Aleppo the next day; the result of Marden's mission gave great satis-

faction to the Turkish Government, the hostile movement was stopped to the rage and disgust of the army,
and Zeitoon was saved.

For this signal service he received the thanks of the
Turkish Governor-General and the English authorities,
and was afterwards appointed by our Government United
States Consular Agent at Marash.

Married Miss Mary L. Cristy, at Brooklyn, N. Y., September 10, 1869; died at Aintab, October 1, 1874; married Miss Alice M. Kingsbury, at Francestown, October
1, 1878, died at Marash, October 17, 1879; married Miss
Ettie C. Doane, of Owasso, Mich., at Marash, December
28, 1882.

Children : Jesse Krekore, nat., March 10, 1872.
Mary L., nat., September 30, 1874.

JOHN WESLEY MILLIGAN, Esq., Pittsburgh, Pa.

John Wesley Milligan, son of Robert and Mary Ann
(Shartess) Milligan, was born at Braddock's Field, (now
Swissvale) Pa., May 15, 1838. His father was a farmer.
He fitted at Wilkinsburg, Pa., and entered college in the
fall of 1858, and continued through the course.

At graduation he was 5-feet 10-inches in height, 145
pounds in weight; had light auburn hair, sandy complexion; was a Republican, a Presbyterian, and intended
to go into business.

After graduation he at once entered upon the study of
law in the office of J. H. Hampton, at Pittsburgh, and
and was admitted to the bar in 1864; practiced law in
the same place till 1876, when he gave it up in order to
carry out his business plans; since that date he has been
connected with the Edgar Thompson Steel Works, the
largest of their class in the country.

His home is at Swissvale, a most charming spot on the Pennsylvania Railroad, eight miles from Pittsburgh, on the farm where he was born, and which has been the family homestead for more than seventy years.

He adheres to the same political and religious creeds as in college days.

Married Miss Mary E. Agnew, at Wilkinsburgh, Pa., July 17, 1866.

Children : Robert, nat., August 28, 1869.
Joseph Frederick, nat., November 13, 1871.
Edwin Irwin, nat., August 27, 1873; ob. March 9, 1874.
Mary Graham, nat., September 14, 1874.
Matilda Carothers, nat., April 9, 1876.
Margaretta Bell, nat., April 9, 1877; ob. March 9, 1881.

REV. JOSEPH ROBERT MILLIGAN, GLOUCESTER CITY, N. J.

Joseph Robert Milligan, son of Robert and Mary Ann (Shartess) Milligan, was born at Braddock's Field, Pa., May 25, 1844. His father was a farmer and coal dealer. He fitted at Wilkinsburgh, (Pa.) Academy, and entered college in the fall of 1858, and continued through the course.

At graduation he was 5-feet 10½-inches in height, 140 pounds in weight, had light auburn hair, sandy complexion; was a Presbyterian, Republican, and intended to engage in business.

After graduation he was engaged in the coal business with his father, in Pittsburgh and Allegheny City, Pa., from 1862 to 1865, residing at the family homestead; from 1865 to 1868 he was a student in the Princeton Theological Seminary, taking the full course of three years. He was then prostrated by a severe sickness of long duration, and by advice of his physician was obliged to indefinitely delay any immediate work in the ministry, and engage in active out-door pursuits. He consequently engaged in the coal business, and afterwards had an interest in the "Iron City Planing Mill," in Pittsburgh.

He continued in active business until 1880, when he went to New York City, where he remained some months in business; in 1881 he lived in Newark, N. J.; from thence to Gloucester, N. J., where he is pastor of the First Presbyterian Church at the present time.

While in Newark he organized the present Young Men's Christian Association. He is a Republican.

He married Miss Mary Elizabeth Marchand, at Pittsburgh, Pa., September 17, 1874.

Children : John Irwin Marchand, nat., Aug. 6, 1875.
Rebecca Conner, nat., November 1, 1876.
Mary Josephine, nat., September 16, 1878.
Sarah Marchand Everson, nat., Apr. 13, 1881.

GEORGE WASHINGTON MORRILL, Esq., ANOKA, MINN.

George Washington Morrill, son of George E. and Hannah (Bartlett) Morrill, was born at Nashua, N. H., June 27, 1836. His father was a physician. He fitted at Kimball Academy, Meriden, N. H., and entered college in 1858, and continued through the course.

At graduation he was 5-feet 7½-inches in height, 160 pounds in weight; black hair, dark complexion, full beard; smoked; paid own college expenses; liberal in creed, Democratic in politics, and intended to become a lawyer.

After graduation, read law with Morrison, Stanley, & Clark, at Manchester, teaching school occasionally till March, 1864; went then to New York City and continued the study of law; was admitted to the New York bar in May, 1864, and engaged in practice of law and real estate business till the spring of 1870, when he removed to St. Paul, Minn., where he pursued his profession for three years; removed to Anoka, Minn., where he has been engaged in the practice of law ever since.

He has been a member of the School Board and also President of the same; has been city attorney and State attorney for his county for four years.

He still clings to his former belief in religion and politics, and says "that there has not been any very remarkable event in my life, but have worked hard and enjoyed good rest at night;" is a Mason.

Married Miss Olive I. Caldwell, at Dunbarton, N. H., December 25, 1866.

Children : Eliza C., nat., Concord, N. H. July 14, 1869.
Mary P. nat., Anoka, October 29, 1874.
George B., nat., Anoka, October 15, 1876.

REV. CHARLES MYRON PALMER, WESTMINSTER, MASS.

Charles Myron Palmer, son of Asa and Pamelia (Rugg) Palmer, was born at Orford, N. H., January 16, 1837. His father was a farmer. He fitted at Kimball Academy, Meriden, N. H.; entered college in the fall of 1858, and continued through the course.

At graduation he was 6-feet 1-inch in height, 180 pounds in weight; had black hair, dark complexion, full beard; was a Republican, a Congregationalist, and intended to become a minister.

After graduation he taught the Hitchcock High School at Brimfield, Mass., from 1862 to 1864; entered the Union Theological Seminary at New York City, in November, 1864; entered Andover Theological Seminary in 1865 and graduated there August 1, 1867; he preached at Harrisville, N. H., from 1867 to 1871; at Cornish, N. H., from 1871 to 1873; at Meriden, N. H., from 1873 to 1881; at Saratoga, California, in 1881-82; and at Westminster, Mass., from March 1883 to date, being pastor of the Congregationalist Church at that place. He has been in ill health since entering the ministry, and was obliged to go to California in 1881 on that account, but has been an actice worker all of the time.

He is a Republican and a Prohibitionist.

He married Miss Marien W. Powers, at Cornish, N. H., August 26, 1868.

No children.

___

EDWIN FRANKLIN PALMER, Esq., WATERBURY, VT.

Edwin Franklin Palmer, son of Aaron and Sarah (Thayer) Palmer, was born at Waitsfield, Vt., January 22, 1836. His father was a farmer. He fitted at Northfield, Vt., and entered college in the fall of 1858, and continued through the course.

At graduation he was 5-feet 8½-inches in height, 145 pounds in weight; had light brown hair, chin whiskers, sandy complexion; smoked; a Congregationalist, a Republican, and intended to become a lawyer.

After graduation he entered the army as Lieutenant in the 13th Regiment Vermont Vols.

In 1864 he began the study of law in the office of Gov. Dillingham, and, after admission to practice, settled in Waterbury, where he has ever since resided in the active practice of his profession.

He has gained a high position as a lawyer at the bar of Vermont, and has been engaged in many important trials.

He represented the town of Waterbury in the State Legislature in the year of 1880, and has taken an active part as a speaker in some of the political campaigns.

In 1880 he was appointed State Reporter of the Supreme Court, which position he still holds, and has published three volumes of the State Reports.

He is a Republican and Congregationalist.

Married Miss Addie D. Hartshorn, of Guildhall, Vt., June 15, 1865.

Children : Edwin F., nat., February 24, 1868.
Annie D., nat., March 23, 1870.
Alice C., nat., May 23, 1872.
Mabel, nat., August 15, 1874.
John H., nat., June 9, 1877.
Charles C., nat., April 8, 1879.

Rev. GEORGE BELA PATCH, WASHINGTON, D. C.

George Bela Patch, son of William and Adeline (Wright) Patch, was born at Hartford, Vt., May 6, 1837. His father was a shoe manufacturer. He fitted at Thetford, Vt., and entered college in the fall of 1858, and continued through the full course.

At graduation he was 5-feet 11-inches in height, 145 pounds in weight; had light complexion, brown hair, side whiskers; paid his own college expenses; was a Republican, a Congregationalist, and intended to become a minister.

After graduation he at once went to Washington, having a call to labor as missionary under the auspices of the First Presbyterian Church of that city.

He received an appointment to a clerkship in the Treasury Department in June, 1863, which he still retains, having been promoted several times.

He pursued a course of theological study, and was called to the pastorate of the Eastern Presbyterian Church of Washington, in 1875, and continued in the same until August, 1881; in the same year he began a new church enterprise in the rapidly growing northwest portion of the city, and as the result the Unity Presbyterian Church was organized, and he was installed pastor of the same April 19, 1882, and so continues.

He has done and is doing a good work, and, as a faithful minister and true Christian, he has the respect and esteem of all who are brought in contact with him.

He made the trip of Europe in the summer and fall of 1878.

He published a volume of poems of much merit a few years since.

He is a Republican, and expresses the belief that he "is thoroughly orthodox, as every Presbyterian clergyman should be."

He married Miss Elizabeth Walker at Washington, January 13, 1864.

No children.

WILLIAM HENRY PECK, CHICAGO, ILL.

William Henry Peck, son of George Clinton and Melinda P. (Wingate) Peck, was born at Lyndon, Vt., January 3, 1841. His father was a farmer. He fitted at Lyndon, and entered college in 1858, and continued through the whole course.

At graduation he was 5-feet 10½-inches in height, 145 pounds in weight; black hair, dark complexion; smoked;

paid his own expenses in college; was a Congregationalist in creed, Republican, and intended to become a lawyer.

After graduation he sold subscription books in Ohio
during the summer and fall of 1862; taught at Union,
Rock Co., Wis., the following winter; taught at Mineral
Point, Wisconsin., from 1863 to 1867, excepting one
year, when he taught at Stoughton, Wis.

He started the "National Democrat," at Mineral Point,
and published the same during 1867 and '68; sold out
and continued teaching at the same place for two years;
in 1870 he bought the same paper and published it till
1874, when he sold out and removed to Chicago in the
fall of that year.

During his residence at Mineral Point he was County
Superintendent and also City Superintendent of schools.
He engaged in the job and book printing business in
Chicago, and so continues, at 119 Clark street.

He is a Democrat in politics and Unitarian in creed.

Married Miss Johanna Hildebrand, at Mineral Point,
October 26, 1864.

Children : Mary H., nat., September 2, 1865.
George C., nat., August 11, 1867; ob. Au-
gust 28, 1868.
Agnes Antonia, nat., January 18, 1869; ob.
April 20, 1871.
Ida H., nat., May 26, 1872.
Etta H., nat., March 12, 1879.

JAY READ PEMBER, ESQ., WOODSTOCK, VT.

Jay Reed Pember, son of Dr. Jacob Read Pember and
Violet (Hidden) Pember, was born at Randolph, Vt.,
September 2, 1841. His father was a physician. He

fitted at the Orange Co. Grammar School, at Randolph, and entered college in spring of 1859, and continued through the course.

At graduation he was 5-feet 11-inches in height, 136 pounds in weight; had light brown hair, light complexion; was a Republican, an Episcopalian, and undecided as to future vocation. During his college course he became an efficient shorthand writer.

After graduation he entered upon the business of shorthand reporting; reported the official proceedings of the Vermont Legislature, in the fall of 1862, and soon after removed to Boston, residing there ten years engaged in reporting.

Being called to Vermont to do the official reporting for the State Courts, he, in 1872, removed to his old homestead in Randolph, where he resided till 1878, when he removed to Woodstock, Vt., and has since resided there.

He is the official short-hand reporter for the courts in Vermont and New Hampshire, being highly complimented by the court and bar for his efficiency, and has reported many of the most important legal cases in New England within late years. Is a Republican and an Episcopalian.

Married Miss Alida Goodwin, of Milwaukee, Wis., September 12, 1866.

Children : Minnie Gertrude, nat., July 26, 1868.

Charles Albright, nat., November 9, 1879.

HON. ALVAH KIMBALL POTTER, LOCKPORT, N. Y.

Alvah Kimball Potter, son of Thomas and Eunice (Marden) Potter, was born at Concord, N. H., March 31, 1840. His father was a farmer. He fitted at Appleton

Academy, Mont Vernon, N. H., and entered college in 1858, and continued with the class till the fall of 1861, when he left to enter the war of the rebellion.

He entered the 7th N. H. Regt. of Vols., as 1st Lieut., in the fall of 1861, and was on duty in Florida and South Carolina till the summer of 1862, when, by reason of disease contracted, he resigned and returned to New Hampshire.

In 1864, having recovered his health, he again entered the military service as captain in the 18th N H. Vols., and went to the front in command of a battalion at City Point, Va.; in the engagement front of Petersburg the Major being killed, Potter was promoted to Major, and was recommended by the Brigade and Division Commanders in general orders for Brevet Rank on account of " gallant and meritorious conduct."

He was on duty in front of Petersburgh till the close of the war, when the regiment was ordered to Washington to do provost duty there, and he was in command of the battalion guarding the assassins of President Lincoln, while awaiting trial.

Studied law at Concord, N. H., and was admitted to bar in 1865, having pursued his studies in 1862-'3, and practiced there three years.

Removed to Niagara Falls in 1868 and practiced there till 1872, when he removed to Lockport, N. Y., and continues his profession to date ; was city attorney in 1876-77, and was elected Judge of Niagara county in 1882 for six years, running largely ahead of the regular Republican ticket.

He has interested himself in scientific matters and delivered some lectures on the same. He is a Republican and a " Congregationalist with liberal views."

Married Miss Ellen S. Fifield, at Concord, July 27, 1865. No children.

GEORGE LOVELL RICHARDSON, Esq., ABINGTON, MASS.

George Lovell Richardson, son of Joseph Lovell and
Sylvia Pond (Patridge) Richardson, was born at East
Medway, Mass., March 9, 1838.   His father was a farmer.
He fitted for college at Monson, Mass., and entered Amherst College in the class of '62; he entered Dartmouth
(class '62) in the fall of 1859, and continued through the
course.

At graduation he was 5-feet 5½-inches in height, 175
pounds in weight; had brown hair, full beard, light complexion; smoked; was a Congregationalist in creed,
Republican, and intended to become a business man.

After graduation he taught in Medway till August,
1864; at Abington, Mass., until July, 1865; then removed to Chicago, Ill., and engaged in the grocery business until September, 1866; then in the lumbering business, at Medway, until April, 1867; then removed to
Abington and became a most successful teacher, and so
continues.

He has been honored with various town offices, and is
a Mason. "Jack" claims to have always been "a most
quiet, peaceable, and law-abiding citizen; a sort of torch
for others to go by; a model husband and father, and a
patriotic citizen generally," and no one of '62 will dis-
pute it.

. He still sticks to the same political and religious creeds
as in 1862.

He married Miss Amelia B. Boyd, at Rockville, Mass.,
December, 1864; ob. July 19, 1879.

Married Miss Alice A. Giles, at Abington, December,
1880.

Children : Joseph Lovell, nat., Medway, Nov. 5, 1865.
Fred. Boyd, nat., Abington, Sept. 1, 1870.

JOHN SANBORN STEVENS, Esq., Peoria, Ill.

John Sanborn Stevens, son of Joshua and Abigail (Walker) Stevens, was born at Bath, N. H., September 16, 1839. His father was a farmer. He fitted at Peacham, Vt., entered college in 1858, and continued through the course.

At graduation he was 5-feet 9-inches in height, 155 pounds in weight; had dark brown hair, side whiskers, light complexion; smoked; was a Congregationalist in creed, Republican, and intended to become a lawyer.

After graduation he taught at Peoria, Illinois, from 1862 to 1864, also reading law with Alexander McCoy of that place; admitted to the bar at Chicago, June, 1865; began practice at Peoria in January, 1866, and has so continued to date; the firm was Mc'Culloch, Stevens, & Wilson, now Stevens, Lee, & Horton.

He has built up a large and important practice, especially in corporation law, being the attorney of the Western Union Telegraph Co., and other corporations.

He was postmaster at Peoria from 1876 to 1880, and has been prominent in political matters. He is a Reformed Episcopalian and a Republican.

He married Miss Sarah M. Bartlett, at Peoria, June, 1868.

Children : Bartlett, nat., 1875.

John S., jr., nat., 1877. Both deceased.

GEORGE HARVEY TAYLOR.

George Harvey Taylor, son of Dr. Samuel Harvey (Dart. 1832) and Caroline Persis (Parker) Taylor, was born at Andover, Mass., June 19, 1840. His father was for many years the head of Phillips Andover Academy.

He fitted at Andover, entered Dartmouth in 1859, and continued through the course.

At graduation he was 5-feet 9½-inches in height, 147 pounds in weight; had brown hair, side whiskers, light complexion; smoked; was a Congregationalist, Republican, and intended to become a lawyer.

After graduation he studied law in Boston with Hon. Lyman Mason (D. C. 1839) and Hon. D. W. Gooch (D. C. 1842,) and was admitted to the bar. In November, 1864 he entered the Army as 1st Lieut., and was mustered out June, 1865; resumed practice in Boston and continued till 1867, when he returned to Andover and became an instructor in Latin and Greek in Phillips Academy; while there, he, in conjunction with his father translated and re-edited Kuhner's Greek Grammar. In 1875 he resigned his connection with the Academy and removed to Nashua, N. H., where he engaged in literary work, and was Justice of the Police Court. In 1877 he became principal of the Kinderhook (N. Y.) Academy; in 1880 principal of the Amsterdam (N. Y.) Academy, and was such at the date of his death. He suffered greatly during the latter years of his life with rheumatism, and died at Amsterdam, June 19, 1881, of rheumatism of the heart. At the time of his death he was making arrangements to publish a new series of Greek text books. He was a member of St. Ann's Episcopal Church, Amsterdam, and, at the time of decease, a candidate for orders in the Protestant Episcopal Church.

He was a most successful teacher, and a man of high character.

He married Miss Jessie Pierce Emerson, of Nashua, N. H., July 8, 1868.

Children : Charles Edward, nat., June 18, 1869.

Harvey Emerson, nat., January 17, 1871.

Caroline, nat., May 2, 1880.

CHAUNCEY WARRINER TOWN, Esq., New York City.

Chauncey Warriner Town, son of Ira Strong and Frances Miretta (Witherell) Town, was born at Montpelier, Vt., July 4, 1840. His father was a merchant. He fitted at Fort Edward, N. Y., entered college in 1858, and continued through the full course.

At graduation he was 5-feet 8-inches in height, 155 pounds in weight; had black hair, mustache, light complexion ; smoked ; was an Episcopalian in creed, Democratic in politics, and intended to become a lawyer.

After graduation he resided at his home at Montpelier, and was Assistant Secretary of the State of Vermont, and Assistant State Librarian from 1862 to 1865; in the meantime he studied law with Hon. T. P. Redfield (Dart., 1836). He went to New York city in 1865, and settled in the practice of law, and so continues, a successful lawyer, at 47 Wall street, New York city.

Never married.

Is an Independent Democrat, and an Episcopalian.

EDWARD TUCK, Esq., New York City.

Edward Tuck, son of Hon. Amos (Dart. 1835,) and Sarah (Nudd) Tuck, was born at Exeter, N. H., August 26, 1842. His father was a lawyer and a Representative of New Hampshire in Congress.

He fitted at Phillips Exeter Academy, entered college in 1859, and continued through the course.

At graduation he was 5-feet 8-inches in height, 132 pounds in weight; had light brown hair, light complexion; was a Congregationalist, a Republican, and intended to become a lawyer.

After graduation he read law in the office of his father at Exeter, during the fall of 1862, but was obliged to give up study on account of trouble with his eyes; he spent the following winter in Louisville and St. Louis; went to Europe in December, 1863 hoping to restore his weakened eyes by rest and travel; entered the United States consular service in July, 1864, at Paris, and became Vice Consul in 1865, and Acting Consul the same year; resigned in May, 1866, and returned to America to engage in active business. He entered the banking house of John Monroe & Co., of New York and Paris, in August, 1866, and became a partner in the same January 1, 1871, which he continued until January 1, 1881, when he retired from active business. While in business he divided his time between New York and Paris, and since then he has traveled very extensively in Europe.

He was very successful in business, and retired to enjoy an ample fortune. He resides at No. 7 East 61st street, New York city.

He is an Independent in politics, and liberal in religious creed.

He married Miss Julia Stell, at St. George's, Hanover Square, London, April 22, 1872, and at the American Chapel, at Paris, France, April 23, 1872.

No children.

DR. JOHN SIDNEY WARREN, NEW YORK CITY.

John Sidney Warren, son of Dr. Moses Roberts and Hannah (Walker) Warren, was born at Middleton, N. H., July 4, 1841. His father was a physician. He fitted at Wolfboro' (N. H.) Academy, entered college in the fall of 1858, and continued through the course.

At graduation he was 5-feet 7-inches in height, 138 pounds in weight; had dark brown hair, light complex-

ion; smoked; was a Congregationalist, Republican, and
intended to become a physician.

After graduation he commenced the study of medicine
with his father at Rochester, N. H.; was principal of the
High School at Rochester, in 1863-'4; at the Portland
Medical School in the summer of the same year; in the
fall (1864) he passed an examination before the United
States Army Medical Examining Board, at Boston, and
received the appointment of Acting Assistant Surgeon,
and served in the 8th U. S. (Col.) Troops, Heavy Artillery,
in Kentucky, and later in Post Hospital at City Point, Va.

Graduated as M. D. at Jefferson Medical College, Philadelphia, in the spring of 1866.

Went into practice at once in New York City, and has
continued to date; his residence is 205 West 38th street.

He has been assistant surgeon for the Ruptured and
Crippled hospital; physician to the Northwestern Dis-
pensary; visiting physician to Alms House and Hospital
at Blackwell's Island, and to other public institutions. Is a
member of the N. Y. Medical Society; N. Y. Obstetrical
Society; N. Y. Academy of Medicine, etc.

He is a Republican and a Congregationalist.

Married Miss Sara Benedict Hutchinson, at New York,
April 23, 1874.

Children : Edward Cyrus, nat., March 6, 1876.
Madeline, nat., October 22, 1877.

DR. AUGUSTUS CHAPMAN WALKER, GREENFIELD, MASS.

Augustus Chapman Walker, son of Joseph A. and
Abigail Walker, was born at Barnstead, N. H., June 9,
1833. His father was a farmer. He fitted at Thetford
(Vt.) Academy, entered college at the beginning of

the course, and left during Junior spring (1861.) He
was given the degree of A. B. with the class in 1871.
While in college he studied medicine with Dr. Crosby
in the winter of 1859-60, and with Dr. Mark Walker
in the winter of 1860-61. After leaving college he attended the Burlington (Vt.) Medical College in summer of 1861 ; Harvard Medical College fall of 1861 and
the spring of 1862 ; at the Soldiers' Hospital, N. Y. City,
from May, 1862 to September, 1862. Asst. Surgeon
133d New York Vols., from September 8, 1862 to September 20, 1864 ; Surgeon of the 18th New York Cavalry
from October 15, 1864 to June 14, 1865 ; attended Harvard Medical School from September, 1865 to March,
1866, when he took the degree of M. D. ; was in N. Y.
City to July, 1866; removed to Greenfield, Mass., and
engaged in the general practice of medicine, which he
still continues, and has been very successful.

He a Republican, and "a Congregationalist of the
mild form."

He married Miss Marcia C. Grant, at Lyme, N. H.,
September 11, 1862.

Children : Robert Turner, nat., October 16, 1867.

Sidney Grant, nat., July 11, 1869.

William Augustus, nat., September 4, 1872.

HON. RANDALL HOBART WHITE, CHICAGO, ILL.

Randall Hobart White, son of Andrew and Lydia So-
phia (Hobart) White, was born at Chesterfield, N. Y.,
May 5, 1833. His father was a farmer. He fitted at
Pembroke, N. H., and Thetford, Vt., entered college
in the fall of 1858, and continued through the full course.

At graduation he was 5-feet 10-inches in height, 170
pounds in weight; had brown hair, light complexion,

full whiskers; smoked; was a Methodist, a Republican, and intended to become a lawyer.

No better account can be given of his life immediately after graduation than as described by himself: " One week after I graduated I found myself in the woods of Mississippi in the neighborhood of Corinth, amid tents and soldiers, with them and among them, but not of them. I was south till the war ended and until March, 1866; was at the battle of Corinth, October 3-4, 1862, and carried a musket; was at Vicksburg for many weeks and at the time of its surrender, and saw much of that historic struggle."

In the spring of 1866 he resumed the study of law at Plattsburgh, N. Y., and in the fall of that year he entered the law school at Albany, N. Y., and was admitted to the bar at Albany, April 6, 1867, and at once went to Chicago, Ill., entered the practice of law, and has so continued.

He represented Chicago in the State Legislature, in the years of 1880-81, and in July, 1883, was, by the Governor of Illinois, on the recommendation of the Judges of Cook county, appointed trial Justice of the Peace for south Chicago, with jurisdiction in matters not exceeding two hundred dollars, and has given great satisfaction, both to the bar and the people, in his judicial determinations.

He has adhered strictly to business, and says that his travels for the past sixteen years have been confined to going from his residence to his office, and returning. He delivered a poem before the annual meeting of the Dartmouth Alumni, at Chicago, in 1882.

In politics he is Republican, and in religion he is " unsettled." His address is 177 Clark street.

Has never married.

DR. AUGUSTUS WISWALL WIGGIN.

Augustus Wiswall Wiggin, son of Henry Lamson and Elizabeth Bond (Wiswall) Wiggin, was born at Wakefield, N. H., June 9, 1841. His father was a merchant and hotel-keeper. He fitted at Phillips Exeter Academy, entered college in the fall of 1859, and continued through the course.

At graduation he was 5-feet 11½-inches in height, 158 pounds in weight ; had dark brown hair, full whiskers, light complexion; smoked ; paid his own college expenses ; was an Episcopalian, a Republican, and intended to become a physician.

After graduation he taught at Belmont, Mass., in 1862-3 ; then studied medicine with Dr. M. B. Warren, at Rochester, N. H., in 1863 ; at Bowdoin Medical College, Me., in 1864, and at Georgetown Medical College, Washington, D. C., graduating M. D. March 2, 1865 ; became a medical cadet U. S. Army, June 17, 1864; assistant surgeon March 15, 1865, and attached to the 5th U. S. Heavy Artillery, June 6, 1865 ; made Brevet Major of U. S. Vols., August 6, 1866, to date from March 15, 1865 ; he then resigned from the army and entered upon the practice of his profession at St. Louis in August, 1866.

During most of 1867-8 he was engaged as acting assistant surgeon in the army of the Department of the Missouri ; appointed assistant surgeon regular army, Nov. 16, 1868, on duty at West Point, N. Y. to December, 1868 ; at Camp Warner, Oregon, to May, 1870 ; ordered to Fort Hall, Idaho, and while on the way he fell from the top of the stage coach and fractured his right leg and severely injured his head, and was carried to Camp Douglas, Utah, and was under treatment till August, 1870, when he went on duty at Fort Stevens, Oregon, and was there to October, 1870 ; at Fort Colville,

Washington Territory, to November 25, 1873; at Fort
Vancouver, Washington Territory, to February, 1874;
at Portland, Oregon, and in the field to July, 1874; at
Fort Stevens to March 7, 1875. He retired about 9 P. M.
on the 6th and was found dead on the morning of the
7th, from the effects of an overdose of chloral, taken to
relieve pains caused by the fall from the coach in 1870,
and from which he suffered to the time of his death.

He was a fine officer with excellent prospects for pro-
motion, and was under orders, at the time of death, to
proceed to the east for examination to the rank of full
surgeon.

NON-GRADUATES.

COL. IRA McLAUGHLIN BARTON.

Ira McLaughlin Barton, son of Hon. Levi W. and Mary A. (Pike) Barton, was born at Newport, N. H., March 11, 1840. His father is a lawyer. He fitted at Meriden, N. H., entered college at the fall term of 1858, and left at the end of the Freshman year.

After leaving college he commenced the study of law in the office of his father at Newport; at the very commencement of the late war he enlisted a company of men, took them to Concord, and was mustered into service, receiving the *first* captain's commission issued in New Hampshire during the war of the rebellion; he was captain of Co. E, 1st N. H. Regt. Vols.; when the term of this regiment had expired (three months) he returned to his home and at once raised another company and was commissioned captain of Co. F in the 5th N. H. Regt., known as the famous "fighting Fifth," and was in many of the most desperate engagements of the war; he was badly impaired in health by exposure during the Peninsula campaign, and was compelled to resign. Having recovered his health he enlisted another company of Heavy Artillery and went in command of the same to Fort Foot, near Washington, as Co. B, 1st Regt. N. H. Heavy Artillery; in 1864 he was sent home and appointed to organize a regiment of artillery, which he did, and was commissioned Lieut. Col., and was stationed in command

at Fort Sumner, near Washington ; was mustered out of
service in the summer of 1865.

Soon after the close of the war he was appointed 2nd
Lieut. in the 28th Regt. of the U. S. Regular Army, and
was ordered to Pine Bluffs, Ark., where he was promoted
to 1st Lieut.; after serving two years he resigned, and
was appointed prosecuting attorney of the 10th Ark.
Judicial District; he remained in this position until he
was appointed Judge of the Criminal Court for the same
district, which office he resigned, and entered upon
the practice of law, and was editor of the " Jeffersonian
Republican," a leading newspaper of that State.

During the eventful troubles in Arkansas known as the
Brooks and Baxter contest, Col. Barton was in command
of Gov. Bishop's troops, and stationed at Little Rock.
One evening, while walking on the public street, a person
whom he had caused to be arrested for a crime a short
time before, came behind him and, unknown to him,
struck him a terrible blow on the head with a heavy re-
volver, felling him to the ground, causing a severe
wound.   He was a long time recovering from its effects,
and it caused him much pain during the remainder
of his life.   After his partial recovery he left Arkansas,
presumably on account of the danger of his living there,
and returned to his home in Newport, in December, 1874,
and engaged in the practice of law with his father; he
never fully recovered his health, and died, after a brief
illness, January 19, 1876.

Col. Barton was a brave man and gained the reputation of being a thorough soldier; he had a warm heart
and was a true friend to all who knew him.

He married Miss Helen M. Wilcox, at Newport, in
1861, who died in 1864.

He married Miss Addie L. Barton, in 1867, who sur-
vives him.

Hon. CHARLES W. CHASE, Clinton. Iowa.

Charles W. Chase, son of Charles and Almira (Moore) Chase, was born at Loudon, N. H., December 8, 1834. His father was a farmer. He fitted at New Hampton, N. H., entered college in the fall of 1858, continued one year, and left at the end of the Freshman year. After leaving college he at once began the study of law with Col. Thomas J. Whipple, at Laconia, N. H., and was admitted to the bar of New Hampshire, in September, 1862; he then enlisted in the 12th N. H. Regt. Vols., was appointed Captain of Co. G, and was in service until the fall of 1864, when he resigned and removed to Clinton, Iowa, and engaged in the practice of law, and so continues.

He has been a member and president of the school board of Clinton; was City Solicitor for four years; Clerk of the District, Circuit, and Probate Courts for four years, and has been for three years and still is, Circuit Judge of the 1st Circuit, 7th Judicial District of the State of Iowa.

He is a Republican, and of no particular religious creed; thinks it would take a long while to tell exactly what he does believe.

He was married to Miss Susan M. Cole, at Lake Village, N. H., September 22, 1862.

Children : Nora W., nat., August 1, 1863 ; ob. August 1, 1864.

Kate M., nat., November 9, 1865.

Charles P., nat., May 15, 1868.

Susan, nat., March 2, 1870.

Vernie, nat., April 1, 1879.

DANIEL CAMPBELL CLARK, Esq., Orford, N. H.

Daniel Campbell Clark, son of Jonathan and Hannah Clark, was born at Orford, N. H., April 25, 1834. His father was a farmer. He fitted at Kimball (Meriden) Academy, and entered college in the fall of 1858, remaining but a part of the fall term, when he was obliged to give up the course on account of his own health and sickness in his father's family.

He has ever since resided at his home in Orford, and is a farmer ; has been selectman two years, and Superintendent of schools for six years.

He is a Republican and a Congregationalist.

He married Miss Sarah M. Richardson, at Hartland, Vt., July 31, 1861.

Children : Leonard N., nat., May 29, 1862.

           Mary A., nat., February 8, 1864.

           George C., nat., April 3, 1867.

WILLIAM Z. COLLINS.

William Z. Collins, son of Stephen Z. and ——(McCoy) Collins, was born in McIntosh county, Ga., in 1840. His father was a lumber manufacturer at Darien, Ga. He entered college in the fall of 1858, and continued through the fall of the Sophomore year, 1859.

After leaving college he returned to his home in Georgia, and was principal of the McIntosh county Academy till the breaking out of the war. While engaged in aiding to fire a salute in honor of the capture of Fort Sumpter, he was most terribly injured by the premature explosion of the cannon, and was confined to his bed for several months, and lost the use of his left arm almost entirely. While confined to his bed he was elected Lieu-

tenant of the McIntosh Dragoons, but could not accept
on account of his injuries; after his recovery he was employed as a tutor for about two years in the family of a
Mr. Spalding, at Darien. In 1863, he entered the
confederate service under the command of the noted
raider, Gen. John Morgan, and served to the close of the
war. He returned to his home, and in 1867 married
Miss Lizzie Bass, who died the following year at the birth
of her child; in 1869 he went to Savannah, Ga., where
he remained for a year and then removed to Sumpter
county, where he lived a few years and then moved
away, and nothing has been heard of him since, and
the general belief among his friends is that he is dead.
He was a Presbyterian and a Democrat.
No children living.

WILLIAM PADDOCK FAIRBANKS, Esq., St. Johnsbury, Vt.

William Paddock Fairbanks, son of Joseph Paddock
and Almira (Taylor) Fairbanks, was born at St. Johnsbury, Vt., July 27, 1840. His father was one of the firm
of Fairbanks & Co., scale makers, at St. Johnsbury.

He entered college in the fall of 1858, and was a member of the class during the Freshman year.

After leaving college he at once engaged in business
with the above firm, and has so continued to date; is now
the treasurer of the world-wide known firm of Fairbanks
& Co., and is an excellent and successful business man.

He represented the town of St. Johnsbury in the Legislature of Vermont in 1881.

He is a Republican and Congregationalist.

He married Miss Rebecca Pike, at St. Johnsbury, April
18, 1861.

Children : Almira Taylor, nat., February 12, 1865.
            Mabel, nat., August 14, 1871.
            Joseph, nat., January 12, 1881.

Hon. HARMON DEWEY FOLLETT, Brainard, Minn.

Harmon Dewey Follett, son of E. D. and Sarah (Bull)
Follett, was born at Bellevue, Ohio, March 17, 1838.
His father was a tanner.   He fitted at Kalamazoo (Mich.)
college, preparatory department, and entered Kalamazoo
college in 1858, and remained through the Sophomore
year; entered the class of 1862, Dartmouth, at the beginning of Junior year, and remained part of that year,
then entered the Junior class at the University of Michigan, where he graduated in 1862; entered the law department of the same institution in 1864, and graduated
in 1866; located at LaSalle, Ill. in the practice of his
profession, where he remained six years, when he was
forced to abandon it on account of bleeding at the
lungs; removed to Ann Arbor, Mich., where he remained three years; since then has lived at Brainerd,
Minn., struggling for restoration of his health, with
varied success.

He is in poor health but has continued his legal pursuits, and has been County Superintendent of Schools,
Court Commissioner, and is now Judge of Probate.

In politics a Republican ; his creed, " Love the Lord
thy God, and thy neighbor as thyself; " is a Mason.

Married to Miss Lillia Morwick, at Ann Arbor, Mich.,
October 23, 1866.

Children : Jamie D., nat., July 6, 1878; ob. August
            18, 1878.

Col. CLARENCE DYER GATES, Cambridge, Vt.

Clarence Dyer Gates, son of Gardner and Clara (Dyer) Gates, was born at Cambridge, Vt., September 23 1839. His father was a farmer and County Judge. He fitted at Fort Edward, (N. Y.) Institute, entered college in the fall term of 1858, and left at the end of Sophomore year.

He enlisted in May, 1861 in the army in Illinois, but the organization was disbanded in August following; enlisted September 1, 1862, in the 1st Vt. Cav., and was made Adjutant of the same October 4, 1862; was A. D. C. on the staff of Gen. Farnsworth when he was killed at the battle of Gettysburg; appointed A. D. C. on the staff of Gen. Custer, to date from September 14, 1863, but was captured at the battle of Culpepper, September 13, and was a prisoner until exchanged May, 1864; he participated in the fights (36 in number) in which his regiment was engaged, when not a prisoner, till the same was mustered out, November 18, 1864.

He was tendered the command of a veteran cavalry regiment being organized at Washington, but the same was disbanded by reason of the close of the war.

He was Inspector and Deputy Collector of Customs in Vermont in 1865-6; was Colonel and A. D. C. on the staff of the Governor of Vermont in 1867-68.

He engaged in trade in 1869 at his old home, and still continues, doing a large business.

He is prominent in the Grand Army Organization, and is the Deputy Grand Commander of the order for Vermont. He is a Republican, a Methodist, and a Mason.

He married Miss Francis. C. VanArnam, at Troy, N. Y., in 1860.

Children : Eugenia, nat., May 6, 1862.

Genevieve, nat., October 7, 1867.

Ardelle, nat., May 19, 1872.

Gardner, nat., April 12, 1874.

EDGAR GLEASON.

Edgar Gleason, son of R. M. and Harriet Gleason, was born at Thetford, Vt., July 26, 1838. His father was the Postmaster at that place. He fitted at Thetford (Vt.) Academy, and entered college in the fall of 1858; he was of a weak constitution, and was taken sick during the winter of 1858, and died at his home in Thetford, January 10th, 1859.

ARTHUR DAVID HAYNES, ESQ., PERRY, KAN.

Arthur David Haynes, son of David and Sarah D. Haynes, was born at Alexandria, N. H., in 1838. His father was a farmer. He fitted at New Hampton, N. H., entered college in the fall of 1858, and continued in the class during the Freshman year.

After leaving college he taught one year at Westport, Mass., and then entered the Law Department of the University of Michigan, and continued two years, graduating L. L. B., March, 1862; then continued the study of law with Hon. Austin F. Pike, at Franklin, N. H., and was admitted to the New Hampshire bar; taught two years at Hastings and Chatfield, Minn., and removed to Perry, Kan., in April, 1866, where he has since resided, engaged in the practice of law, and interested in farming.

He is a Republican, and Independent in creed.

Married to Miss Amelia F. C. Hoad, at Lecompton, Kan., in 1868.

Children : Marcus Haynes, nat., December, 1869.
          Hugh, nat., March, 1872.
          Sarah G., nat., July, 1874.
          Arthur, nat., May, 1881.

HON. ORVILLE RINALDO LEONARD, CARSON, NEV.

Orville Rinaldo Leonard, son of John and Lois Leonard, was born at Gaysville, Vt., November 13, 1834. His father was a farmer. He fitted at Randolph, Vt., entered college in the fall of 1858, and left college in the fall term of the Junior year, 1860.

After leaving college he at once went to California and commenced the study of law with the firm of Belcher & Belcher at Marysville; was admitted to the bar in May, 1863; went to Humboldt, Nev., and engaged in practice; was elected District Attorney in 1863, and held the position until 1869; was a delegate to the Chicago Convention in 1868, which nominated Grant; was elected Judge of the Supreme Court of Nevada in 1876, for six years, and was re-elected in 1882 for a term of six years more. He ranks as one of the ablest lawyers on the Pacific coast; has published several volumes of the Nevada Supreme Court Reports.

He enjoys a salary of $7,000 per year.

He is a Republican and has taken an active part in the political affairs of his State; in religious faith he believes in the Overruling Providence, and that we cannot escape punishment for wrong doing, but in no other sense does he believe in eternal punishment.

Married Miss Eliza B. Sylvester, of West Newbury, Mass., at Stockbridge, Vt., May, 1868.

No children.

DR. JOHN CLAY McKOWEN, CAPRI, BAY OF NAPLES.

John Clay McKowen, son of John and Elizabeth (Langford) McKowen, was born at Jackson, La., in 1842. His father was a merchant and planter, and lived mostly in Paris, France. He fitted at Mt. Holly and Elizabeth City, N. J., entered college in 1859, and continued until the summer of 1861, when he left at the breaking out of the civil war.

After leaving college he returned to his home in Louisiana, and entered the Confederate service, became Lieut. Colonel of the 15th Confederate Cavalry, and as such was in active service until the close of the war.

He made a good reputation as an able and daring officer; among other things, he, with five men, entered the Federal lines at Port Hudson, during the memorable siege of 1863, and captured General Neal Dow and his guard while in their headquarters, and carried them inside the confederate lines and sent them to Libby prison at Richmond.

After the close of the war he returned to Dartmouth, and graduated with the class of 1866.

He then went to Europe and became a student of medicine at Paris in 1866-7; returned to America in 1868, bought a ranche in California and became a ranchero at Los Angeles, and was elected the Alcade; in 1870 he sold out and removed to San Francisco and became Vice Principal of the public schools in that city in 1870-72. In 1872-76 he was a student of medicine, at Vienna, Austria, and Munich, Bavaria, taking his degree of M. D. at Munich; engaged in the practice of medicine at Rome, from 1876-78, when he was taken with malarial fever and went to Capri, in the Bay of Naples, for his health, and was so attracted by the beauties of that earthly paradise that he has resided there ever since. He has a fine villa, has a vineyard and olive orchard, and occupies his time in writing, painting, making oil and wine, for a portion of the year, and travels the rest, spending his winters in Egypt, Greece, Tunis, Southern Spain, and other localities.

He has published a history of Capri, which is a valuable authority, historically, and interesting to the reader. He has never married.

A southerner in political faith, and seems to think that his religious tendencies are " Buddhism mixed with the maxims and precepts of our old college friend Horace." His life seems to have fallen in pleasant places, and he appreciates and enjoys it accordingly.

SAMUEL JONES MORRIS, Esq., DeWitt, Iowa.

Samuel Jones Morris, son of James L. and Agnes E. Morris, was born at Morgantown, Penn., June 16, 1839. His father was a merchant. He fitted at Fort Edward, N. Y., entered college in the fall of 1858, and remained through the Sophomore year, being obliged to give up his studies on account of his eyes.

After leaving college he at once " went west " and settled at Princeton, Scott county, Iowa, where he remained until October, 1882, when he removed to DeWitt, his present residence. His own words will best describe his life.

" My life, since my eyes forbade my continuance with the boys of 1862, has been mainly spent in bucolic pursuits, in the ' *otium cum dignitate* ' of farm life, although I am free to confess the ' *otium* ' was not at all times discernible to the naked eye. As a relaxation therefrom the —' *otium*,'—I spent some years with moderate constancy and fair success as a teacher, and take rather pardonable pride in the style and manner of ' fitting ' which I gave several young men for college. I had thought that the ' *tupto, tupso, tetupha*,' the ' *arrecti comœ*,' and all that, had gone off on a tangent, and had well nigh hoped it had, and have only to thank one young man, half Irish, half German, and wholly polyglot, for the novel discovery that it had not wholly gone, and it is fitting that I bid welcome to what is left."

' In October, 1882, he removed to DeWitt, Iowa, where he is the head of the firm of Morris, Barr, & Morris, patentees and manufacturers of the " Iowa Cyclone Hub Borer," which will bore a set of wheels in forty minutes, which kind of cyclone we hope will pay him better than a small-sized one did last July, that swept his farm, about $2,000 worth, in less time.

He has filled responsible positions, such as Assessor, Collector, Justice of the Peace, Census taker, &c.; also, was interested in the publication of a history of Scott county, furnishing much of the material. He is a Republican and an Episcopalian.

He has a firm belief in "matches made in heaven," as he says that "Mrs. M. and myself have the same measure of years, days, hours; twins, so to speak."

He married Miss Eleanora V. L. Corney, at Davenport, Iowa, February 5, 1863.

Children : Eleanora V. L., nat., July 3, 1864.
'Agnes E., nat., May 14, 1868.

GILMAN NOYES, ESQ., ATKINSON, N. H.

Gilman Noyes, son of Hazen and Lois (Hayford) Noyes, was born at Atkinson, N. H., March 8, 1839. His father was a farmer. He entered college in the fall of 1858, and was in college one year, leaving at the end of Freshman year.

He remained at home until he entered the war of the rebellion, enlisting April, 1861, in the 1st Regt. N. H. Vols., and remained until the regiment was mustered out

of service, August 9, 1861; re-enlisted in the 7th N. H.
Regt. Vols., October 5, 1861, and was discharged November 9, 1864; he was wounded in the right shoulder in the engagement at Olustee, February 20, 1864.

After his military service he remained at home for a season, then went west, where he engaged in business; then returned to Atkinson November, 1867, and studied law in Haverhill, and also in Boston, but was obliged to give it up on account of physical difficulties, and has been engaged in farming ever since.

He is a Democrat and an Episcopalian.

He was married to Mrs. Caroline S. Nelson, of Haverhill, Mass., at Atkinson, January 3, 1884.

RETIRE HATHORN PARKER, Esq., BOSTON, MASS.

Retire Hathorn Parker, son of Retire H. and Hannah (Chase) Parker, was born at Exeter, N. H., January 2, 1840. His father was a tanner. He fitted at Phillips Exeter Academy, entered college in the fall of 1858, and continued until the Sophomore year, when he was compelled to relinquish his studies on account of ill health.

After leaving college he went on a sea voyage which benefited him greatly; after that he entered a store in Boston, where he remained two years; he then engaged in the sugar refining business, and was the Superintendent and Manager of the well known " Union Sugar Refinery" at Boston, Mass.

In 1878 he left the refining business and established a mercantile house at No. 4, Liberty Square, Boston, which he still continues.

He has resided in the Charlestown District in Boston since 1862.

He is a Republican, and Congregationalist "orthodox" in creed, and " has always paid one hundred cents on the dollar, and has got some left."

Married to Miss Caroline D. Pollard, at Charlestown, March 5, 1872.

Children : Mary Ednah, nat., March, 1873; ob. November, 1874.

Edith, March, 1874.

Helen Livingston, nat., October, 1875.

Marion, nat., November, 1879.

Caroline, Margery, (twins,) nat., June, 1883.

SAMUEL PORTER PUTNAM, Esq., New York City.

Samuel Porter Putnam, son of Rufus A. and Frances H. Putnam, was born at Chichester, N. H., July 23, 1837. His father was a Congregational clergyman. He fitted at Pembroke (N. H.) Academy, entered college in the fall of 1858, and left college during Junior year to enter the army.

He entered the 4th N. Y. Heavy Artillery, and was connected with the same until he passed a competitive examination before the Military (Casey's) Board at Washingington, and was appointed Captain in the 20th U. S. Colored Troops, and served until the close of the war. After the war he studied theology at Chicago, Ill., was ordained a Congregationalist (orthodox) minister in 1868, and preached three years; then entered the Unitarian ministry and preached at Toledo, Ohio, one year; at Omaha and North Platte, Neb., three years; Northfield, Mass., two years; Vincennes, Ind., one year, and then left the ministry and accepted a position in the Custom House at New York City, which he still retains.

He has written some remarkable productions which

have attracted much attention and caused much comment
in literary circles; they are the "Golden Throne," and
"Prometheus," and several others of the liberal order;
no better commendation can be given of their excellency
than was expressed by the late Dr. Bellows, who, in
speaking of "Prometheus," said, "it is crammed with
life, thought, and profound emotion, poured forth, it
seems to me, with extraordinary richness and beauty;"
and the Century, "the value of the work lies in the vigor,
consistency, and eloquence with which the moral temptations of to-day are set forth;" and Col. Ingersoll, speaking of the "Golden Throne," "the author certainly has
genius; the divine creative spark is within him."

He is a Republican, and an "Agnostic" in religion.

He married Miss Louise Howell, at Chicago, May 1st,
1868.

Children : Harry, nat., May 1, 1869.
Gracie, nat., April 29, 1871.

JOHN J. SANBORN, Esq., Washington, D. C.

John J. Sanborn, son of John and Laura S. Sanborn,
was born at Charlestown, Jefferson county, West Virginia, September 6, 1840. His father was a teacher. He
entered college in the fall term of the Sophomore year,
1859, and left college in 1860.

After leaving college he returned to his home in Virginia, and entered the Confederate army; he left that
service and came into the Federal lines, and has resided
in Washington since 1863, where he has been engaged
in various departments of the Government, and so continues, being employed at the present time in the office
of the Commissioners for the District of Columbia.

He gives no sketch of himself, saying, that "life is too short," and that he has held no offices of any kind, has had no degrees, never married, never made any import- ant travels, or engaged in anything of interest belongs to no political party, and has no religious belief.

REV. ARTHUR HUBBARD SOMES, WEST BARNSTABLE, MASS.

Arthur Hubbard Somes, son of Benjamin and Ruha- mah French (Stevens) Somes, was born at Laconia, N. H., January 24, 1835. His father was a mason and contrac- tor. He fitted at New Hampton, N. H., entered college in the fall of 1858, and left at the end of the Junior year, (1861).

Directly after leaving college he was engaged as asso- ciate principal of the Blairstown (N. J.) Presbyterial Academy, a classical school, where he aided in fitting many students for Princeton, Yale, and Lafayette; here he remained two years; he then entered the Princeton Theological Seminary, and was a student two years, when he was ordained and installed pastor of West Con- gregational Church at Warren, Mass., September 18, 1865, where he served till 1869; then returned to Blairstown and took charge of the classical department of the same institution that he was formerly connected with, remain- ing four years; was elected principal of the Newton Col- legiate Institution, N. J., but declined, and taught a few pupils as private tutor for two years; supplied the Pres- byterian Church at South Bethlehem, Pa., 1875-7: the Congregational Church at West Warren, Mass., 1877-82; then removed to Barnstable, Mass., where he now re- sides.

He received the honorary degree of A. M. from Prince- ton College.

Has taken an interest in educational matters, and served on the school Boards of different places; is now supervisor of schools for Barnstable.

He is a Republican and a Congregationalist.

Married Miss Helen A. Bodfish, at Barnstable, in 1863.

Children : Helen Adelaide, nat., 1868.
        H. Roy Blair, nat., 1874.
        Arvilla May, nat., 1878.

ALGERNON SYDNEY SYMMES.

Algernon Sydney Symmes, son of Robert Symmes, was born at Ryegate, Vt., February 22, 1838. He fitted at Kimball Union Academy, Meriden, N. H., and entered college in the fall of 1858.

He was taken with what proved to be a fatal illness in the summer of 1859, and died in September, 1859, at his home at Ryegate.

NOAH LANE MERRILL,
AFTERWARDS JOHN ARTHUR TEBBETTS.

Noah Lane Merrill, son of Noah L. and Malinda (Tebbetts) Merrill, was born at Northfield, N. H., in 1838. His father was a store keeper. He fitted at Tilton, N. H., entered college in the fall of 1858 and left at the end of the Sophomore year, (1860).

During the last term of the Freshman year he had his name changed to that of John Arthur Tebbetts, a relative promising that he would provide the means for his education and starting in business, in case he took that name.

He went to New Haven and entered the law school,

but the promised aid failed, and he was greatly in need; he was attacked with typhoid fever, and died (date unknown) and was buried at the public expense.

CHARLES HENRY TIBBETTS, Esq., FRYEBURG, ME.

Charles Henry Tibbetts, son of Charles and Drusilla (Richardson) Tibbetts, was born at Fryeburg, Me., July 22, 1841. His father was a dealer in lumber and real estate. He fitted at the Fryeburg Academy, entered college in the fall of 1859 and left at the end of the spring term of the Sophomore year (1860) on account of trouble with his eyes, which still continues.

After leaving he engaged in business at Fryeburg as a merchant, and has continued to the present time. In 1866 he entered the lumber and real estate trade in connection with his other business.

He is a Republican, and liberal in creed.

Married Miss Hattie C. Cummings, at Norway, Me., November 8, 1869.

Children : Ellen F., nat., November 24, 1870.

Edith L., nat., December 15, 1872.

CHANDLER SCIENTIFIC SCHOOL.

WILLIAM HENRY BALDWIN, Esq., YONKERS, N. Y.

William Henry, son of David and Amanda M. (Hobbs) Baldwin, was born at Nashua, N. H., March 10, 1842. His father was a manufacturer. He fitted at Kimball (Meriden) Academy, entered the Scientific School at the fall term of 1859, and completed the course.

After graduation he entered the Army as Lieutenant in the 1st New York Vol. Engineers, served at Hilton Head and at the seige and capture of Morris Island, and in the Army of the James, in front of Richmond and Petersburg till the close of the war, when he was mustered out as Captain.

Since then he has been engaged in the general practice of Civil Engineering, at Yonkers, N. Y., where he still resides.

He was the Chief Engineer in designing and constructing the sewerage works of Memphis, Tenn., Norfolk, Va., Buffalo, N. Y., and other cities.

In 1881-2 he collected the social statistics for the 10th Census of the U. S., examining and reporting upon the sewerage and sanitary works of New York, Philadelphia, Chicago, Cincinnati, Pittsburgh, Louisville, &c.

He is a Republican, a Baptist, and a Mason.

Married to Miss Helen Adele Reed, at Nashua, N. H., October 25, 1872. No children.

Dr. GEORGE EDWARD DARLING.

George Edward Darling was born January 17, 1840, at St. Stephen, New Brunswick.

After graduation he pursued the study of medicine, and graduated at the Dartmouth Medical College in 1866; was in the Hospital at Manchester, N. H. for some months, and then settled in the practice of his profession at Erie, Pa.

He was attacked with typhoid fever and died from its effects at Erie, in 1868.

PROF. JOHN ROBIE EASTMAN, NAVAL OBSERVATORY, WASHINGTON, D. C.

John Robie Eastman, son of Royal F. and Sophronia (Mayo) Eastman, was born at Andover, N. H., July 29, 1836. His father was a farmer. He fitted at New London, N. H., entered the Scientific School at the fall term of the Junior year (1860), and completed the course.

After graduation he taught a private school at Wilmot, N. H. until November, 1862, when he was appointed an Assistant in the U. S. Naval Observatory at Washington, D. C.

He was appointed Professor of Mathematics in the United States Navy, February 17, 1865, with the rank of Lieutenant Commander. He has been engaged in Astronomical work since 1862, and now has charge of the Meridian work at the Observatory, and has edited the annual volume of Astronomical Observations since 1874. He observed the total solar eclipse of August 7, 1869, at Des Moines, Iowa; was sent by the United States Government to observe the total solar eclipse at Syracuse, Sicily, in December, 1870, and visited the principal observatories of Europe; made similar observations at Las Animas, Colorado, in July, 1878.

He was in charge of the party to observe the transit of Venus, December 6, 1882, at Cedar Keys, Forida.

He has published a number of papers on Astronomical subjects, but most of his productions are printed in the annual volumes of Observations, published by the U. S. Naval Observatory.

He has received the degree of Doctor of Philosophy, (Dartmouth, 1877); is a fellow of the American Association for the Advancement of Science, and is General Secretary of the same; also is a member of the Washington Philosophical Society.

He is "Independent" in politics.

He is President of the Dartmouth Alumni Association of Washington, and through his efforts the largest and most successful meeting of Alumni was held last February that ever met at the annual banquet in Washington.

He married Miss Mary Jane Ambrose, at Boscawen, N. H., December 25, 1866.

No children.

Dr. CHARLES MELROY FELLOWS.

Charles Melroy Fellows was born at Thetford, Vt., June 4, 1831.

After graduation he studied medicine, and graduated at the Bowdoin (Me.) Medical School, in 1865. Was in the Douglas General (Army) Hospital, Washington, D. C. as Hospital Steward during the latter part of the late civil war.

Settled in the practice of his profession at Lawrence, Mass., where he died in 1876.

He married Miss Esther S. Wright, of Bethel, Me., March 15, 1864.

VALENTINE P. FERRIS.

Valentine P. Ferris was born at Swanton, Vt., September 15, 1840.

After graduation he became a commercial agent, and removed to Indiana. He was lost in a snow storm on the plains near Fort Hays, Kansas, while hunting buffalo in the winter of 1874.

He married Miss Lou Harrell, of Cincinnati, Ohio, July 9, 1867.

WILLIAM HENRY FESSENDEN, Esq., Boston, Mass.

William Henry Fessenden, son of Abijah and Louisa M. Fessenden, was born at Buffalo, N. Y., July 26, 1840.

His father was a plumber. He fitted at Boston, Mass., entered the Scientific School in the fall term of 1858 and continued to the fall term of the second class (1860).

After leaving college he was purser of the Boston and Philadelphia Steamship Co. until the Government took their vessels for transports, at the breaking out of the war in 1861; enlisted as a private in Co. L, 1st Mass. Cavalry, in November, 1861; was severely wounded at the battle of Pocotaligo, S. C., October 22, 1862, and was in hospital at Beaufort, S. C. till April 23, 1863, under treatment, when he was discharged on account of disability; after discharge he remained at his home at Hyde Park, Mass., an invalid for a year or more; upon recovery he entered the employ of the American Telegraph Co., and afterwards was in that of the Western Union Co. as Auditor of the Eastern Division, with his office in Boston; in 1874 he resigned and devoted himself to the profession of music, which he has since followed.

He was for some years one of the most prominent members of the famous " Boston Ideal Opera Troupe," and traveled over much of the United States and the Canadas.

He is a Republican, " of no settled religious belief," a Mason of the 32d Degree.

His residence is No. 30, Milford street, Boston.

He married Miss Harriet A. Sunderland, at Philadelphia, in 1860; ob. 1875.

Married Miss Mabel B. Burnham, at Boston, in 1876.

Children : Louisa Ewins, nat., 1861.

Alice Harriet, nat., 1865.

LEANDER MILLER HASKINS, Esq., ROCKPORT, MASS.

Leander Miller Haskins, son of Moses and Betsey D. Haskins, was born at Rockport, Mass., June 20, 1842. His father was a mariner. He fitted at Andover, Mass., entered the Scientific School in the spring term of 1860, and continued through the course.

After graduating he continued the study of engineering and surveying in Boston; taught in the winter of 1862-3; went to New Orleans in May, 1863, and joined the 19th Army Corps, as Commissary Chief Clerk, stationed at Port Hudson and Carrolton; discharged by reason of sickness in September, 1863; appointed clerk in the Navy Department in December, 1863; resigned in April, 1866; continued the study of engineering in Boston until October, 1866, when he was reappointed a clerk in the Navy Department; resigned in October, 1868, and entered into a partnership with his brother Moses W. Haskins, in the wholesale fish and oil business; in November, 1879 he engaged in the manufacture of isinglass, and so continues.

He is "Independent" in politics, and a Congregation-
alist in creed; also a Mason and Knight Templar.
Has visited the Pacific coast.
He married Miss Gertrude Davis, of Chicago, at Bos-
ton, December 19, 1871.
No children.

CHARLES CURTIS HEILGE.

Charles Curtis Heilge was born at Boston, Mass.,
July 8, 1841.
After graduation he became an assistant engineer in
the U. S. Navy. After the war he went into business in
Boston, where he died in 1871.
He married Miss Annie Rand, of Hanover, N. H.

HON. JOHN HOPKINS, MILLBURY, MASS.

John Hopkins, son of James and Elizabeth Hopkins,
was born at Leonard Stanley, Gloucestershire, England,
March 19, 1840. His father was a fuller. He fitted at
Phillips (Andover) Academy, entered the Scientific School
in the fall of 1858, and continued through the course.
After graduation he began the study of law with Joseph
B. Cook, at Blackstone, Mass., and was admitted to the
Massachusetts bar in March, 1864; began the practice of
law in Millbury, in 1864, and practiced there and in
Worcester ever since, having offices in both places; has
a good practice in both civil and criminal law; has been
twice a member of the Massachusetts Legislature, (1882
and 1883) and held important chairmanships of commit-

tees. He has been Selectman, School Committee, Assessor, Trustee of Library, Treasurer of the Episcopal mission, &c.

He says, " Haven't had time to travel; haven't published anything. I don't know whether or not my classmates will be glad to know it, but as a matter of fact, I have been the defeated candidate of the Democratic party for Congress, (9th Mass. Dist.), for State Senator, for District Attorney, and for State Auditor."

He married Miss Mary C. Salisbury, of Blackstone, Mass., November 21, 1864.

Children : Grace E., nat., January 17, 1866.
Paul Fenner, nat., March 12, 1867 ; ob. August 6, 1867.
Herbert Salisbury, nat., February 5, 1868.
John Earl, nat., February 14, 1869 ; ob. August 4, 1869.
Herman Phillips, nat., January 22, 1873.

JOHN A. STAPLES, ESQ., REVERE, MASS.

John A. Staples, son of James H. and Sarah E. (Dudley) Staples, was born at Lyman, Me., September 5, 1841. His father was a grocer. He fitted at the Biddeford (Me.) High School, entered the Scientific School in the fall of 1868, and continued through the full course. After graduation he was engaged in business at home for two years; in 1864 he went to Buffalo, N. Y., in the interest of the Shaw & Clark Sewing Machine Co., and remained there two years, then transferred to Chicago, where he was two years, when he closed his connection with said company and made an engagement with the Union Paper Collar Company, of New York. Returning to Biddeford was elected City Clerk in 1870, which office

he held till 1873, when he was appointed cashier of the
Eastern Railroad Corporation, with headquarters at Boston, which position he still retains.

He resides at Revere, a few miles out of Boston.

He is one of the Selectmen of the town of Revere, and
gives great satisfaction. He was the Superintending
School Committee of Biddeford, for three years.

He is a " Jeffersonian Democrat " in politics, and a
" Conservative Orthodox " in creed.

He married Miss Josephine Goodwin, at Biddeford,
December 5, 1867.

Children : Walter Henry, nat., August 28, 1870; ob.
January 30, 1877.

Phillip Clayton, nat., October 24, 1882.

SAMUEL WELLES.

Samuel Welles was born December 15, 1841, at Glas-
tenbury, Conn.

After graduation he was appointed an assistant at the
Naval Observatory in Washington, August, 1862, and
resigned the same in October of the same year. Was
appointed a civil engineer in the U. S. Navy in 1862, and
was on duty at the Washington Navy Yard and afterwards at the New York Yard. He was then ordered on
duty at the Mare Island Navy Yard, California, where he
died July 10, 1866, from injuries received from the explosion of the boiler of a portable engine.

He had an excellent reputation as engineer and as an
officer.

He never married.

EDWARD BENTLEY YOUNG, Esq., Boston, Mass.

Edward Bentley Young, son of Edward and Harriet E. Young, was born at Reading, Mass., June 29, 1841. His father was a mechanic. He fitted at the Reading High School, entered the Scientific School at the beginning of the third year (1859) and continued through the course.

After graduation he began the study of medicine, but concluded to teach. Taught at Gloucester, Mass., in the winter of 1862-3; at Winchester in 1863; at South Amesbury, Mass., in 1864-66; then at Boston, where he has since continued. Was junior submaster of the Brimmer School 1866-68; senior submaster of the same 1868-76; master of the same 1876-80; master of the Prince School from 1880 to date.

He has devoted much time to the study of the sciences.

He is prominent in the Odd Fellow Brotherhood; is a Mason of the 32d Degree, and has held many high positions in the order.

He is a Republican and an Episcopalian.

His residence is 104 Appleton street.

He married Miss Ella L. Bird, at Boston, October 1, 1873.

No children.

RECAPITULATION.

Academic.	Living.	Deceased.	Total.	
Graduates............	50	7	57	
Non-Graduates...........	16	4	20	
				77
Scientific.				
Graduates........	6	5	11	
Non-Graduates...............	....	....	15	
				26
Total........	....	....	103	

www.ingramcontent.com/pod-product-compliance
Lightning Source LLC
Chambersburg PA
CBHW030625270326
41927CB00007B/1318